# CRUSADERS FOR FREEDOM

# CRUSADERS FOR FREEDOM

*by*

*Henry Steele Commager*



ILLUSTRATED BY MIMI KORACH

*Doubleday & Company, Inc.*
*Garden City, New York*

LIBRARY OF CONGRESS CATALOG CARD NUMBER 62–15876

PRINTED IN THE UNITED STATES OF AMERICA

To
STORM JAMESON

*"Knowing the secret of happiness to be freedom*
*and the secret of freedom a brave heart,*
*not idly to stand aside from the enemy's onset."*

CONTENTS

We are the music-makers,
And we are the dreamers of dreams,
Wandering by lone sea-breakers,
And sitting by desolate streams;
World-losers and world-forsakers,
On whom the pale moon gleams:
Yet we are the movers and shakers
Of the world for ever, it seems.

With wonderful deathless ditties
We build up the world's great cities,
And out of a fabulous story
We fashion an empire's glory:
One man with a dream, at pleasure,
Shall go forth and conquer a crown;
And three with a new song's measure
Can trample an empire down.

We, in the ages lying
In the buried past of the earth,
Built Nineveh with our sighing,
And Babel itself with our mirth;
And o'erthrew them with prophesying
To the old of the new world's worth;
For each age is a dream that is dying,
Or one that is coming to birth.

ARTHUR O'SHAUGHNESSY

# FREEDOM OF SPEECH

REPEAL OF THE STAMP
PLATO
UNCLE TOMS CABIN
COMMON SENSE
INHABITANTS
AMERICA
SUBJECTS
AGE OF REASON
LIBERATOR
DAILY TIMES
FREE PRESS

What is the most important of all rights?

Well, that is a hard question. It is like asking what is the most important part of school, the teachers or the pupils? It is like asking what is the most important part of an automobile, the engine or the body? The fact is that all rights belong together and that you can't very well have some of them without the others. No teachers—no school; no pupils—no school either. No engine—no car; no body—no car either.

Still, if somebody took you by the throat and pushed you against a wall and made you say what right came *first*, there is no doubt how you would respond. You would yell. You would say, "Let me go. You can't make me tell." And there you are: that is the first right—the right to yell; the right to speak up, or not to speak up if you don't want to; the right to be heard.

It may not be the most *important* right, but it is the *first* right.

Why? Very simply, because without it you can never get any of the others. After all, if you can't make yourself heard, if you can't speak up, you won't get any rights at all. No use talking about the right to worship God in your own way if you can't even pray without someone breathing down your neck. No use talking about the right to an education if your teacher can't call his soul his own and if you can't read anything that the police haven't passed on first. No use talking about a fair trial if you can't have a lawyer to help you or if you can't tell your own story in court.

Free speech and free press—the right to be heard and the right to hear—this is the first right because all the others depend upon it.

So let us begin with this one.

Let us begin with Tom Paine, over in England. Not always in England; eventually he threw in his lot with the Americans. But in England when he made his great fight for the right to be heard.

Poor Tom Paine! He wasn't much to look at, with his big nose and his ears sticking out and his shoulders all hunched up, and his clothes looking as though he had slept in them. He wasn't much anyway. He was a failure at everything he tried, one of those unfortunate people life had marked out for a failure. He wasn't even allowed his full name. Everybody says Thomas Jefferson, but nobody ever says Thomas Paine; it's just plain Tom Paine. Everything he put his hand to went wrong, somehow. He left school at thirteen, and after that he educated himself on the run. He signed up as a sailor but he never did like sailing, or the sea, and soon gave that up. He was a corset maker, and he hated that job—what young man wouldn't? He even got a job as tax collector, but he couldn't for the life of him keep his records straight and pretty soon he was out of that job too. He was born and bred a Quaker, but he couldn't manage to be a good Quaker, and what with one thing and another he had to drop out of that church. . . . No wonder Tom Paine decided to leave England and try life in the New World.

Somehow he had managed to meet Benjamin Franklin while he was in England. The kindly Dr. Franklin gave him letters to friends over in Philadelphia, saying that he was an "ingenious, worthy young man." So off Tom Paine went, across the Atlantic, to America.

Maybe there was something in the air of the New World that agreed with Mr. Paine. At any rate, as soon as he landed in Philadelphia—and that was at the close of the year 1774—he began a new life. The Tom Paine who had been a failure at everything was forgotten, back there in England. Now there was a new Tom Paine—a young man who almost overnight became a great man.

Now how did that happen? It wasn't just the American air that did it, though that helped. It was the times as well. Tom Paine was one of those men—you find a good many of them in the pages of history—who jog along being nobodies in ordinary times but come to life in time of trouble. He was made for trouble. Give him a nice pleasant life in a pleasant little village with a pleasant wife and children and a pleasant dull job, and he would be just a pleasant dull little man. But war, or revolution, or crisis, sent an electric current right through him, from tip to toe.

When Tom Paine landed in Philadelphia in December 1774 the air was full of electrical currents. That very year delegates from all parts of America had come to the City of Brotherly Love to plan—well, to plan a revolution. The next spring Minutemen stood at Lexington Common and Concord Bridge, up in Massachusetts, and "fired the shots heard round the world." And with that the war was on—the war for American independence and for freedom.

What a time to be in America! For that matter, what a time to be alive! It was all meat and drink for Tom Paine.

Now he was in his element. War! Independence! The rights of men! Every day Paine got more excited, and every day he grew an inch or two.

But somehow everybody else wasn't as excited about war and independence as Mr. Paine. That would never do. He was going to fight, all in good time, but first he had to win Americans over to independence. He fought that fight with his pen—and what a pen! Others could use swords and guns better than Tom Paine but nobody could use a pen better. He made his pen into a whole battery of guns; he made it into a whole army of swords. He sat down and wrote a little book—not nearly as long as this book—but what a book! *Common Sense,* he called it. How silly, he said, that a continent should belong to an island; common sense that it should be independent. How silly that kings should rule over men; common sense that men should rule themselves. . . . And then that stirring plea at the end:

> O! ye that love mankind. Every spot of the old world is overrun with oppression. Freedom hath been hunted round the globe. Europe regards her as a stranger, and England hath given her warning to depart. O! receive the fugitive, and prepare in time an asylum for mankind.

What a book. It swept over America like a prairie fire. Soon everybody in America who could read was reading *Common Sense,* and if they couldn't read they learned to read just for that. Soon everybody in England was reading it too—everybody who could read, and that wasn't a very large number. And everybody who read it said, "Of course! That is the *common sense* of the matter. Of course America ought to be independent." In no time at all poor Tom Paine, who had once made corsets, had made a revolution and a new nation too. Not all by himself, of course: George Washington had something to do with it, and Thomas Jefferson, and Patrick Henry, and many others, but in his way Tom Paine did as much as any of them.

It wasn't just a matter of writing *Common Sense*. It was one thing to declare independence and another thing to whip the British redcoats who came pouring over, shipload after shipload. By now Paine was in Washington's army, but that didn't mean that he stopped writing. Not at all. There he was, marching through the snows of a Northern winter, the poor soldiers leaving bloody footprints when they walked, and everybody frozen and starving while the snow came down and the wind howled and the British disported themselves in front of their warm fires in New York City. So once again Tom Paine took his quill pen in hand, and made a writing desk out of a drumhead, and wrote away for dear life:

> These are the times that try men's souls. The summer soldier and the sunshine patriot will shrink from the service of their country, but he that stands it *now* deserves the love and thanks of man and woman.

He called his paper *The Crisis*. Tom Paine was made for crises. All through the war he wrote one crisis paper after another, until in the end Lord Cornwallis had to surrender, there at Yorktown, with the redcoats playing "The World Turned Upside Down" and Tom Paine writing, "The times that try men's souls are over." Thanks to all who had fought through those long hard years, and thanks to Tom Paine, who had fought with sword and pen.

After that things were dull for Mr. Paine: He lived for revolution and crisis. The Americans had had their Revolution and had won their rights. Perhaps there would be other revolutions—and other rights to win.

Sure enough there were. A few more years and the French started a fire that swept across the whole of Europe, flaming and burning for twenty-five years, and changing the history of the world. The French people who had for so long suffered and groaned under tyranny threw off the burden of the ages. They got rid of king and queen, of counts and marquises and all the rest. Soon poor Louis XVI had his head chopped off, and his queen Marie Antoinette too. They weren't bad people, they just had the hard luck to get in the way of a revolution. Soon the soldiers of France were swinging down the roads to nearby countries across the Rhine singing that new song from Marseilles:

*Arise, ye sons of Liberty,*
*The day of glory has arrived!*

It wasn't all glory; for that matter it wasn't all liberty either. But that is another story.

You can imagine how excited Tom Paine was. He was in England when word came that the people of Paris were storming through the streets of their city, opening the gates of the prisons and shouting for liberty. "Where Liberty is not, there is my country," said Paine, and over he went, to Paris, to be in on the Revolution. The French were so pleased to see him that they made him an honorary citizen.

Mr. Paine was already a citizen of the United States, but he was delighted to be an honorary citizen of France as well. Still and all, what he was really most interested in right now was not France. What he was most interested in now was England.

The Americans had had their Revolution and had won their freedom. Now the French were having their Revolution too, freeing men from serfdom and ignorance and giving them the rights of men. But what of England? What of England?

What indeed? Over in England kings and princes, lords and ladies, with their great palaces and country houses, with hundreds of servants at their beck and call, with money to waste and food to waste and lives to waste, were lying awake nights wondering if it would be their turn next. And over in England, too, hundreds of thousands of poor farmers and miserable workingmen and humble preachers and scribblers and lawyers were lying awake nights wondering if maybe it would be *their* turn next—their turn at last to have enough to eat for themselves and their children, and shelter from rain and snow, and enough work to go around, and a chance to send their children to school, and to worship as they wished, and to have some say in the kind of government they had. A chance, in short, at some of the rights that Americans had won for themselves and that the French were even now winning.

That was what Tom Paine was asking too. When would his fellow Englishmen win some of the rights of men? Back he came to England to see what he could do about it. Back he went to his writing table, and his pen flew so fast it almost burned through the paper and into the desk. Then he wrote "Finis." And he called his book *The Rights of Man.*

Just simply that: *The Rights of Man.*

*The Rights of Man* was another book like *Common Sense* and *The Crisis.* It talked about men as men, not as rulers and subjects. It said that men could govern themselves and that all men had equal rights.

What dangerous ideas! What a dangerous fellow. He had been dangerous in America, he had been dangerous in France, but there was nothing the English could do about that. Now he was dangerous in England, and there was something they could do about that. Put him down! Arrest him and throw him in the Tower of London. Put his book down! Arrest anyone who sold it or anyone who read it. And as for the book itself: Burn it! Gather up all the copies and make a big bonfire of them and burn them to ashes. That would teach Tom Paine to come back to England with his terrible ideas.

They tried to arrest Paine but he had already slipped away, back to France again. Back to prison, as it turned out, for the wheel of the French Revolution had taken another turn, and now Tom Paine was much too peaceful and mild for its leaders. The English tried to put him in prison because he was too radical, and the French put him in prison because he wasn't radical enough. It's certainly hard to please everybody, thought Tom Paine.

But let us leave poor Paine sitting in his cell in the jail in Paris wondering if maybe he shouldn't have stayed in America after all. Let us leave Paine and go back to England.

Back in England they were getting ready to fight France. But somehow they had time for Tom Paine and his terrible book anyway. Even the Prime Minister, William Pitt, had time for that. If they couldn't get Mr Paine—the French had done that for them—they could at least get his book. Make an example of it! Teach people not to write books like that—teach them not to have ideas like that.

Back then to England, where the mighty William Pitt has put Tom Paine and *The Rights of Man* on trial.

It is more than Tom Paine who is on trial.

It is more than his book which is on trial.

It is freedom of speech and freedom of the press which is on trial.

All the great powers of England are determined to stamp out these freedoms. Who dares stand up for freedom?

"I dare," said Thomas Erskine.

There may have been greater lawyers in the history of England than Thomas Erskine—lawyers who knew more of the mysteries of the law, lawyers who could draw up better wills or better contracts, or talk more learnedly about bailments and torts.

But never was there a more eloquent lawyer.

Never was there a more courageous lawyer.

Thomas Erskine was so eloquent that when he talked the winds stopped blowing so they could hear him and then carry his words around the world. He was so eloquent that when he talked it was like hearing a whole symphony orchestra.

And he was just as courageous as he was eloquent. He had the heart of a lion. Nothing could daunt him, nothing could silence him. He would look a Lord High Chancellor in the eye and say just what he believed. He would call the Prime Minister of England and put him in the witness box just like anybody else. He would defy the King himself.

And all this eloquence and all this courage he gave to the cause of freedom.

He was really a nobody to start with, Mr. Erskine, even though his father was an earl; not a nobody like Tom Paine, but certainly not one of the great swells who ruled England and Scotland in those days. He was a poor Scots boy, and like Tom Paine he had enlisted in the navy and knocked about the world, seeing all sorts of queer things and places, and having all sorts of things happen to him. Once he was even struck by lightning, and survived: it took more than a bolt of lightning to kill Tom Erskine. He stumbled into the law entirely by accident—just happened to be in court one day and was so fascinated by it all that he decided then and there to be a lawyer himself. So off he went to college, at twenty-five—how embarrassing for him—and then to the study of law. When he was almost thirty he was a full-fledged lawyer and ready to take cases if anybody wanted him. For a long time nobody did. But then, again quite by accident, he stumbled into his first case and came out of it a famous man. For in it he dared to attack one of the most powerful lords in the kingdom—the man who was in command of the British navy. Even you know his name: it is Lord Sandwich. Yes, that is where the lowly sandwich comes from: Lord Sandwich was so busy playing cards that he couldn't even stop for dinner, so they invented the sandwich for him, and named it after him too. But that's all the good he ever did in the world. Tom Erskine proved that it was Lord Sandwich's fault that the ships of the royal navy were falling apart and the food was mouldy and the sailors were deserting by the hundreds.

After that Tom Erskine had more cases than he knew what to do with. But he didn't take just the cases of the great and the rich, though these came pouring in on him. He took the cases of the poor and the helpless. And what he liked best were those cases in which the government was trying to silence somebody or put down somebody.

Like Admiral Keppel, who was tried for losing a battle.

Like John Stockdale, who was arrested and tried for publishing a criticism of the House of Commons.

Like the poor publisher who had dared print an almanac without permission.

Like the Quakers who were persecuted for their faith.

Like Tom Paine—and *The Rights of Man.*

Now the government had put Tom Paine on trial for his life—and his book too. And there was Mr. Erskine in his long black silk robes and his white wig standing up to speak for Mr. Paine.

There wasn't a great deal he could do about either Mr. Paine or *The Rights of Man.* Mr. Paine wasn't there to speak for himself. And as for *The Rights of Man,* the judge and the jury were convinced that it was a very dangerous book. Thomas Erskine did his best. He spoke of the rights and the liberties of Englishmen—of the right to speak and to read, and of freedom for those who spoke up or those who wanted to learn. He talked about freedom for ideas that were dangerous as well as freedom for ideas that were safe.

Here is a hard lesson to learn.

Safe ideas don't really need freedom, because nobody ever bothers about them. Nobody will ever question your right to talk about the weather. Nobody will ever try to stop you from talking about a football game or a cricket game. No judge will ever lock you up because you read the comics or the sports page of the newspaper.

No, it is only dangerous ideas that need freedom. Or ideas that some people think are dangerous. . . .

The jury and the judge thought that Mr. Paine's ideas were dangerous. For when Erskine was through the jury said "Guilty" and the judge said "Guilty."

If Tom Paine had been there they would have put him in jail—or maybe hanged him. But he wasn't there. He was still in France—writing another book.

That wasn't the end of *The Rights of Man,* not by any means.

Flushed with victory, Mr. Pitt decided to punish everybody who printed the hated book, and everybody who read it, and everybody who dared express the ideas that were in the book.

Then a reign of terror began.

John Frost was arrested and dragged off to jail because he had published *The Rights of Man.*

The editors of a newspaper were arrested and sent to jail because they had advertised *The Rights of Man.*

Up in Edinburgh, in Scotland, a small group of men held a meeting to talk about the right to vote. In marched an army of soldiers and swept them all off to jail.

Back in London the members of a club to study politics met and passed a resolution that "all government is instituted for the general good," and then went from bad to worse by passing another resolution saying that everybody had a right to an education. That was really too much! Members of that club were arrested and so, too, were the editors of the paper that dared to print the resolutions.

Then there was a poor shoemaker named Thomas Hardy (you will think everybody was named Thomas, and you are almost right). He got above himself and organized a society called the Friends of Freedom, and dared to make a speech saying that the government of George III was wicked and corrupt.

Who did Thomas Hardy think he was, anyway, to criticize the government and the King of England?

He was arrested too.

Never had Mr. Erskine been so busy. Everybody came to him for help, and he took all their cases. The other lawyers were afraid, but not Thomas Erskine. All the judges in the land couldn't scare him.

One by one the government brought all its victims to trial. Lawyers for the government painted Mr. Frost and Mr. Hardy and the others as desperate men, bent on revolution. You would suppose, to hear the lawyers talk, that they all had horns on their heads and cloven hoofs. You would imagine that they were all going around with daggers between their teeth and torches in their hands, ready to kill and to burn.

But then Mr. Erskine stood up and his voice was now soft and pleading, like a violin, now sweet and piercing, like a flute, now mighty and thundering, like an organ when all the stops are pulled out. He talked about freedom and what it meant. He talked about justice and how precious it was. He talked about the rights of Englishmen, and how dearly they had been won, down through the ages. He talked about the rights of man.

The jurymen sat there and listened, and their hearts beat twice as fast, and their eyes brightened, and they drew hope and courage from him. And when Mr. Erskine was through they stood up and said in a loud voice, "Not guilty!" Time after time, case after case, "Not guilty!" The publishers, the speakers, the rebels and reformers, were *not guilty!* Not guilty, Your Honor! Not guilty, my lords. Not guilty, O people of England!

The judges and the ministers gnashed their teeth in rage, but all over England plain men and women lit bonfires to celebrate Tom Erskine and his victories.

Almost singlehanded he had stopped the reign of terror. Almost singlehanded he had saved freedom of speech and of the press in England.

Remember that poem by James Russell Lowell:

*They are slaves who dare not be*
*In the right with two or three!*

In the right with two or three! Between them, Tom Paine and Thomas Erskine struck a mighty blow for freedom. One of them wrote *The Rights of Man.* The other made it possible for people to read it. Together they made it more than a book, they made it a living force.

But of course no rights are ever won for all time. They have to be won over again by each new generation of men.

You would think if there was one place in the world where the rights of free speech and free press were safe it was the United States.

That's where you would be wrong.

Look now to the city of Boston. It is a dark December day in the year 1830, and a tall thin young man—already bald and old-looking—is sitting in a cellar room, writing away by the light of a flickering lamp. He is William Lloyd Garrison. He is writing a letter "To the Public," which he is going to publish in the very first number of his new magazine, the *Liberator*. As you can guess from the title, it is a magazine to stir up the people against slavery.

> I am in earnest. . . . I will not excuse. . . . I will not retreat a single inch. . . . I WILL BE HEARD!

The first number came out on the first day of the new year, and after that it came out every week. Every week Mr. Garrison spoke his mind, and every week he was *heard.*

How they hated him in the South. But they couldn't do much about it there. . . . And how they hated him in Boston, too, for stirring up trouble.

You would have thought that he was not a quiet, peaceful, religious man but a firebrand, stirring up a revolution, the way they talked about him.

Come to think of it, that is just what he was doing. He was making a revolution. For what a revolution it would be, to do away with slavery!

They tried to starve Garrison out.

They tried to destroy his press.

They seized him and pulled him through the crooked streets of Boston with a rope around his neck, as if they were taking him to the gallows. That's what they wanted to do, too.

But "I will be heard," Garrison had said, and he was heard, year after year. Nothing could silence him or his paper, neither hostility nor poverty. In time Boston got used to him. In time Boston came almost to admire him, he was such a persistent fellow, so firm and so courageous. And Boston liked courage. So Mr. Garrison went on publishing his newspaper and speaking his mind.

Other editors who fought slavery weren't so lucky.

Look west and you will see what happened to a young man out there who thought slavery wicked and was determined to say so.

The young man was Elijah Lovejoy. A good biblical name, Elijah—one you don't hear much any more. He had a good religious upbringing, listening to his father preach every Sunday, and reading the Bible every night until he knew it by heart, and took it to heart, too. He had grown up in Maine and gone to one of those little New England colleges that have sent out so many young men to become great men. Then, like thousands of others, Elijah heard the call of the West. There was nothing much for him to do in

Maine, so he thought, while out west there was everything to be done.

So off Elijah went, a young man of twenty-five, to the distant frontier of Missouri, to the bustling river town of St. Louis. What a lively place it was—fur trappers back from a winter's hunting in the Rocky Mountains, and steamboats puffing upstream, their decks loaded with bales of cotton and black smoke pouring out of their smokestacks, the Negro stevedores running up and down the narrow gangplanks loading and unloading and loading again for the downstream run. . . . Negro slaves everywhere, for Missouri was one of the states where people still had slaves.

Young Mr. Lovejoy got himself a job on a St. Louis newspaper, and in no time at all he became editor. That ought to have satisfied him, but not at all. He got to worrying about his soul—what a worrier this young man was anyway!—and went back east to Princeton to study religion and to become a minister. Then back to St. Louis again; now he could preach as well as edit a paper. Not that the two were so very different, for Mr. Lovejoy was always preaching, no matter what he did.

Picture him, then, bustling about St. Louis and the countryside of Missouri and Illinois, just at the time when tall lanky Abraham Lincoln was growing up in Illinois and wondering about slavery too. Lovejoy kept his eyes open as he went about Missouri, and he didn't miss much. What he saw mostly was slavery, because you see what you are looking for. Lots of people who lived in Missouri or, for that matter, in Alabama or Georgia, right in the middle of slavery, didn't see it at all—it was like a piece of furniture that had always been there.

Yes, what Elijah Lovejoy saw was slavery. Slavery in Missouri, slavery across the river in Kentucky, slavery everywhere in the South. Slaves up and down the great river, working on the steamboats, along the levees, working for other people—never for themselves. Every day he read his

Bible, and every week he read Mr. Garrison's newspaper, the *Liberator*. Gradually he came to the conclusion that slavery was wrong—against religion and against morals. Well, a good many people had come to that conclusion. But Lovejoy was like Mr. Garrison back in Boston: he thought he ought to do something about it.

But surely not here in Missouri, where all the best people owned slaves! It would stir things up; it would make trouble. So when Lovejoy began to talk about slavery there were black looks and mutterings, and then his readers and some of his parishioners began to say, "If you don't like it here, why don't you go back where you came from? Why do you come out here and make trouble? *We* don't mind slavery—why should *you*?" And soon the men who owned the paper that Lovejoy edited took him aside and told him that he must find something else to worry about—something nice and safe and far away like the Greeks or the Italians, but not slavery. There was a mass meeting of the citizens of St. Louis just to discuss Mr. Lovejoy. They too thought that Mr. Lovejoy should stop talking and writing about slavery. Of course he had a right to speak his mind—everybody had a right to do that—but not about slavery. Let him speak his mind about other things. Free speech was all very well, but it meant free speech about nice safe things that didn't bother anybody, not about dangerous things that were bound to stir up trouble.

But Mr. Lovejoy was a hard man to deal with. He wasn't easily scared. When they came to him and told him to be quiet or go away, he held a kind of mass meeting of his own. Listen to him as he stands there, a tall straight young man, telling the people of St. Louis what was the meaning of freedom of speech:

> The truth is, my fellow citizens, that if you give ground a single inch, there is no stopping place. I deem it therefore my duty to take my stand upon the Constitution. Here is firm ground. . . . I do therefore as an American citizen, and a

> Christian patriot, and in the name of Liberty and Law and Religion, solemnly protest against all these attempts to frown down the liberty of the press. . . . I declare it to be my fixed purpose to submit to no such dictation. And I am prepared to abide the consequences. I have appealed to the laws of my country. If they fail to protect me I appeal to God and with Him I cheerfully rest my cause.

As it turned out, it didn't do Mr. Lovejoy much good to appeal to the laws. One night a St. Louis mob decided it would teach Mr. Lovejoy a lesson; it descended on his shop, seized his printing press and scattered it around the countryside. Lovejoy could take a hint, all right, and he decided to leave St. Louis.

But he wasn't running away; he was made of sterner stuff than that. He just moved across the river to the town of Alton, in Illinois, and there he set up his newspaper all over again and prepared to make things as uncomfortable for the St. Louis slaveholders as he could. Soon he had a new printing press and a new paper, and the citizens of St. Louis were reading just what they had read before.

But somehow Mr. Lovejoy was meant for trouble. The people of Alton, Illinois, turned out to be very much like the people of St. Louis, Missouri. They believed in free speech and a free press . . . but not when it meant stirring up trouble. Why stir up trouble? So now it was an Illinois mob that broke into the Lovejoy office and threw his press into the muddy waters of the Mississippi. There, that would take care of the troublesome Mr. Lovejoy!

Of course it did no such thing. There wasn't a more stubborn man west of the Alleghenies than Elijah Lovejoy, and in hardly any time at all he had himself a new press and new type and was at it hammer and tongs every week. . . . It was more than the people of Alton could stand for. All they wanted was peace and quiet; all they wanted was to be left alone. Why couldn't Mr. Lovejoy write about pleasant things, instead of writing about slavery all the time?

What a nuisance this young man from Maine was, anyway.

So one hot day in the summer of 1837 there was another mass meeting, and now it was the people of Alton, Illinois, who told Mr. Lovejoy either to shut up or to shut up shop. He had worn out his welcome—if he ever had any. Now would he please be quiet or go back home.

Neither, came Mr. Lovejoy's answer: neither. So that very night a mob of Alton citizens descended on the Lovejoy office and smashed it up and then decided to smash up Lovejoy himself while they were at it. He came out and faced them. "I am in your hands," he said. "You can do with me what God permits you to do." They left him and went home.

Now it was a real contest of wills. The whole city was up in arms—the mayor, the townspeople, everybody said, "Go home, Mr. Lovejoy, and leave us in peace." But "I pledge myself to continue my newspaper until death," said Mr. Lovejoy. "If I fall my grave shall be in Alton." For the third time he sent off for a new press. For the third time his friends raised money and bought a press and sent it on to him, down the long, winding Ohio River and up the Mississippi River on one of those great puffing steamboats. Mr. Lovejoy and his friends went down to the docks to meet the boat and to unload the new press and carry it to a warehouse, and there they stood guard over it as the short November day turned to night.

And that night the mob gathered again. This time it meant business. This time it was going to silence that troublemaker forever. The mob surrounded the warehouse and started shooting. Then it advanced on the warehouse to set it afire. Lovejoy rushed out to put out the fire; there was a shot, and he fell dead. The rest of the defenders gave up and went home, and the gleeful mob found the press and threw it into the river to join its cousins already down at the bottom of the waters.

It was quite a victory.

That was the end of Elijah Lovejoy.

That was the end of his press.

That was the end of the agitation against slavery in Illinois.

That would teach editors a lesson—teach them not to interfere with folks, not to write about unpleasant things, not to make trouble.

No such thing. If that had really been the end of Elijah Lovejoy, why do you think you would be reading about him now?

Let's turn back to Boston, where we left William Lloyd Garrison publishing the *Liberator*.

Like a thunderclap came the word that Elijah Lovejoy had been killed defending the freedom of the press.

He was the first martyr to a free press in the history of the country—the first man to give his life for the right to speak out and the right to be heard.

No wonder Boston was aroused. Even those who didn't care one way or the other about slavery cared about free speech. What is more, they decided to *do* something to show how much they cared. They decided to call a great meeting in Faneuil Hall and pay tribute to the martyred Lovejoy. But when they asked the mayor for permission to use the hall he got cold feet and said no.

That looked as if Boston was as bad as Alton, Illinois—afraid of free speech. That would never do, said old John Quincy Adams; he had been President of the United States, and now he was in Congress fighting for the right of everybody to send in petitions and have them read—freedom of speech in Congress, freedom of speech in Boston! That would never do, said the Reverend William Ellery Channing. He was Boston's most beloved minister, a saint if ever there was one, and when he raised his gentle voice nobody could resist him: after all you can't resist a saint.

So the mayor gave in, and one wintry day in December

thousands of Bostonians crowded into ancient Faneuil Hall to protest the murder of Elijah Lovejoy. It was a good place to come to, Faneuil Hall. It had been built by a refugee from tyranny who had found freedom in Boston—the French Huguenot Peter Faneuil. It was called the Cradle of Liberty, and that was a good name for it, for it was here that Boston had listened to Sam Adams and James Otis and other leaders of the Revolution as they denounced the tyranny of George III and spelled out the nature of American liberty.

Look at the scene this December day. There was old John Quincy Adams sitting in the very middle of the platform, a tiny little man: he was seventy years old now, but still full of fire. And next to him gentle, frail William Ellery Channing—only a few more years to live, and all of them devoted to good works. And thousands of men and women crowded onto the floor and jammed into the galleries. And hanging from the walls, looking down on the great crowds, paintings of the Fathers of the Revolution.

Then came the speeches praising Lovejoy, and the resolutions about free speech and free press. But not so fast! Who was this working his way to the front? It was James Austin. A first citizen, James Austin—an overseer of Harvard College and the attorney general of Massachusetts, and all the other proper things you can think of. Now he got up to speak and there was silence. He didn't hold with all this nonsense about Lovejoy, he said, and he didn't hold with all this talk about slavery either. If Mr. Lovejoy had just kept quiet about slavery nothing would have happened to him. As it was, said Mr. Austin, it was all Lovejoy's fault. "He died as a fool dieth," said Attorney General James Austin.

There was a stunned silence. Then up stood a young man named Wendell Phillips. Like Mr. Austin, he was a member of the first families—you have heard of *Phillips* Exeter and *Phillips* Andover academies—and everybody knew him. "Can you stand thunder?" said old President Adams to Mr.

Channing. And thunder there was, and lightning too—such eloquence as had rarely been heard even in that famous hall. At the height of his speech Wendell Phillips stopped and pointed to the long row of paintings hanging from the walls of the galleries, paintings of the great patriots of the past. "I thought those pictured lips would have broken into voice to rebuke the slanderer of the dead," he said. "For the sentiments he had uttered, on soil consecrated to the prayers of Puritans and the blood of patriots, the earth should have yawned and swallowed him up."

A new hero had emerged, a new leader in the never ending struggle for freedom. For almost fifty years Wendell Phillips was to give his life to the cause of freedom—freedom for the Negro slave, freedom for women, freedom for workingmen, freedom of speech and of the press. He was a rich young man, and he could have lived a life of ease, but he chose instead a life of service to mankind. "Don't shilly-shally, Wendell," his invalid wife would say to him as he left for one of his speeches, "don't shilly-shally." Never did Wendell Phillips shilly-shally, never in a long life dedicated to the rights of man.

So you see the mob in Alton, Illinois, didn't really win after all. They killed Elijah Lovejoy, but they couldn't kill the things he lived for and the things he died for. Nobody remembers the members of that mob now. Nobody even remembers Alton, now, except as the place where Elijah Lovejoy printed his paper and the place where he was killed. He carried the torch of freedom, and when he died it was seized by others before it could fall to the ground and flicker out. It was taken by Wendell Phillips, not braver but more eloquent. And Wendell Phillips carried on the fight that Lovejoy had begun. He lived to see the end of slavery. He lived to become a great man in Boston. After he died Boston put up a statue to him, and Alton put up a statue to Elijah Lovejoy.

# FREEDOM OF RELIGION

Of all the rights that men have worked for and fought for, it is the right to worship God that has mattered most. There are only two ideas that men have been willing to die for: one is country, and the other is religion. But to fight and die for your country can't really be called fighting for a right; it is more like fighting to live. To die for religion, though—that is to die for an idea . . . for a right.

But why in heaven's name should people have to die for their religion? If there is one thing that is private, it is religion. If there is one thing that doesn't really concern other people, it is the way you pray, or the way you think about God and about your own soul.

The odd thing is that, although everybody wants *his own* private religion, there are always some who won't let other people have *their* private religion. "I must worship God as I please," they say . . . and, "you must worship God as I please, too. Religion is private—for me, but not for you!

"You must worship our way, or we will punish you.

"You must believe what we believe or we will burn you at the stake.

"You must say what we say, or we will tear your tongue out of your mouth.

"You must go to our church, or we will tear down your churches.

"You must bring up your children to worship the way we worship, or we will take them away from you."

All religions teach peace and kindness and mercy. Yet for hundreds of years men have waged war and tortured and burned and killed, all in the name of religion.

What a paradox!

But there have always been some who went right on believing that they had a right to worship as they wished—that religion was a private matter, and nobody could tell them what they should believe. There have always been some men—yes, and women too—who would stand up for their religion no matter what the cost. They were ready for the hard looks and the hard words, they were ready to be beaten and even tortured, they were ready to give up everything they owned and everything they held dear, even life itself, in order to worship God their own way.

The Pilgrims . . . the Puritans . . . Roger Williams . . . Lord Calvert and the Catholics . . . William Penn and the Quakers . . . the Huguenots from France . . . Scots Presbyterians from the Highlands . . . Jews from Portugal—look at them as they crowd onto the ships that will carry them to America, where they can worship in peace.

But don't think that religious liberty is just American. It didn't even begin in America. It began in Holland, before there was any America—any English America, anyway.

But it was in America that it was planted most deeply and that it grew and spread.

Now why do you suppose that was?

Was it because Americans were so much wiser than other people?

Was it because they were so much better than other people?

No, of course not. People are pretty much the same everywhere—some are wise and some are stupid, some are good and some are bad.

The reason that Americans made such a success of religious freedom is really very simple. It was because they had to.

After all, men and women of every faith came to America. Those who first came to Virginia were members of the Church of England. Those who went to Massachusetts Bay were Puritans. Those who sailed for Maryland were Catholics. To Pennsylvania went Quakers and Lutherans and Brethren and others. North Carolina attracted the Highland Scots, and they were, of course, Presbyterians. And Huguenots from France (we shall hear more about them later) and Jews from Portugal and Spain scattered all through the colonies. If you were to paint a map of the colonies with each religion in a different color it would look like a patchwork quilt.

Now suppose each one of these religious groups had said, "Our religion is the right religion, and yours is all wrong. If you worship our way, you will go to heaven, but if you worship your way you are sure to go to hell. We don't want you to go to hell, so we shall do you a favor and *make* you worship our way."

Just suppose each of them had said that—Puritans in Massachusetts and Baptists in Rhode Island and Quakers in Pennsylvania and Presbyterians in North Carolina and all the others as well. . . . Everybody fighting everybody else. Everyone at his neighbor's throat. There would have been no government, not even any religion, for how can government or religion flourish in the midst of hatred and war?

It is common sense to let people alone, common sense to allow to others the same freedom you want for yourself. And after all, America was a big country . . . much bigger than any of the countries of the Old World. If you couldn't stand the way other people worshiped, you could always go off and settle down somewhere on the frontier and worship the way you wanted to.

What good luck that America was so big!

Good luck for Roger Williams, certainly.

Some people are born to religion, just as some people are born to music or to painting. You could no more keep Roger Williams away from religion than you could keep little Wolfgang Amadeus Mozart away from a piano or young Benjamin West away from a canvas and a box of paints. It was something that filled his whole life. And he wouldn't take anything for granted, either; he wouldn't take any ready-made religion. He had to make it himself. He went to all the right schools—to the old Charterhouse School in London, to the ancient university of Cambridge along the River Cam, and he studied all the right things so that he became a learned man, but all the time what he was thinking about was God and religion.

In due course of time Roger Williams became a preacher. But of course he had to preach his own way.

Needless to say, there was no room for him in England, not in the days when King James and King Charles sat on the throne, back in the 1600s. They weren't going to stand any nonsense about people having their own religion. There was a perfectly good religion already—the Church of England, it was called. It was good enough for the King, and it was good enough for all the lords and ladies, and it was good enough for the bishops; certainly it was good enough for plain men like Roger Williams. If you didn't like the Church of England you'd better keep quiet about it, or you'd end up in jail, or something worse.

That is, you would unless you were clever enough to get out. . . .

But where to go?

Some Englishmen who wouldn't join the Church of England went off to Holland and settled in "the fair and beautiful city of Leyden." But after they had lived there ten or twelve years they found that their children were growing up Dutch instead of English—what did they expect?—and were being drawn off into other religions. So these Pilgrims —for that is what they were called—decided to go to the "vast and unpeopled countries of America." So in 1620 "they left the goodly and pleasant city which had been their resting place; but they knew they were pilgrims, and looked not so much on those things but lifted up their eyes to the heavens, their dearest country." Off they went, across the great ocean in the little cockleshell ship, the *Mayflower,* to the sandy shores of Cape Cod, and founded the colony of Plymouth.

There were only a hundred or so Pilgrims off to America to find a place where they could worship in peace, but ten years later there were a thousand who were ready to follow them across the Atlantic, a thousand men and women and children. And before they were through there were no less than twenty thousand: ship after ship bobbing its way across the ocean to the distant shores of Massachusetts Bay. And of all of them we can say what the Pilgrim William Bradford said:

> Being past the vast ocean and a sea of troubles, they had now no friends to welcome them, nor inns to entertain them or refresh their weather-beaten bodies, no houses, or towns, to repair to, to seek for succor. And for the season it was winter, and they that know the winters of that country know them to be sharp and violent and subject to cruel and fierce storms. What could they see but a hideous and desolate wilderness, full of wild beasts and wild men? And what could now sustain them but the spirit of God and His Grace?

Roger Williams was one of those who "hungered and thirsted after righteousness." All his life he sought righteousness . . . and never quite found it.

Most people are finders. Early in life they find what they want, or maybe just want what they find. They find their religion and it satisfies them. They find their work and stick to it cheerfully enough. They find what they believe in politics, and after that they never give the matter another thought. They find what they like in painting or in music, and then they say, "I don't know much about it, but I know what I like."

But some people are born seekers. They spend all their life seeking something. Oftentimes they don't know what it is they are looking for—some beauty, some goodness, some knowledge. Some, like Christopher Columbus, are seekers after new continents. Some, like the astronomer Galileo, are seekers after new worlds in the skies. Some, like little Wolfgang Amadeus Mozart, are seekers after new beauty in music. And some, like Roger Williams, are seekers after new truths.

In 1630—he was just twenty-seven years old—Roger Williams decided to follow the other Puritans to the New World. One dark December day he and his wife went aboard the little ship with the big name, the *Lion*, and off they sailed, up and down through the winter gales and the winter waves for two months, before they made safe harbor in Boston. Roger Williams began to preach at once. Almost everybody was preaching in Massachusetts Bay in those years, and those who weren't preaching were going to church to listen to sermons: a wonder they found any time to get any work done! Then up to the little town north of Boston with the biblical name of Salem—a few unpainted frame houses huddled together on a sandy spit of land sticking out into the ocean. It was a wonderful place for sailing and for fishing, but in Salem too everybody was so busy writing sermons or preaching them or listening to them and talking about them that they really had very little time for sailing and fishing. Not yet, anyway. The time was to come when Salem would be the greatest sailing town in all America, but that was still a long way off.

So there was Roger Williams, studying and preaching and trying to find out what was the truth. In Salem everybody liked him and admired him—well, almost everybody—but down in Boston they took a very different view of it all.

What was this they heard, down in Boston? What was this Mr. Williams was saying?

He said that religion was a private matter.

He said that the government had control over the bodies of men but not over their minds or their souls.

He said there were lots of things the governor and the magistrates and the ministers down in Boston didn't understand, and that they hadn't any right to force their ideas on the people of the colony.

And then on top of that he said all the land belonged to the Indians anyway, and the colonists ought to buy it from them and pay them a proper price for it.

No wonder the governor and the magistrates and the ministers in Boston all shook their heads. This would never do. This Roger Williams was upsetting everybody with his newfangled ideas. He was disturbing the peace.

He must be silenced.

The Puritan Fathers were good and wise men, most of them, but there was one lesson they still hadn't learned. When King Charles of England had told them how they should worship God, they had up and left for Massachusetts Bay. Now they were telling everybody in Massachusetts Bay how *they* should worship God. They had not yet learned that what is sauce for the goose is sauce for the gander. They had not learned that it was just as wrong for them to be intolerant toward others as it was for others to be intolerant toward them. They had not learned the golden rule of freedom—that if you would be free you must allow others to be free.

Roger Williams was getting ready to teach them that lesson.

One day the judges and the ministers told Mr. Williams to come down to Boston and explain himself. Nothing he liked better than that! Down he came, and soon he and the Boston ministers were at it, back and forth, one argument bang up against another argument.

In the end, of course, the Boston ministers had their way. They said that Mr. Williams was preaching dangerous doctrines and disturbing the peace. So, out with him! If he wanted to preach a lot of nonsense let him go somewhere else and do it. Not in Salem. Not in Boston. Not in the Massachusetts Bay Colony.

It was January, the snow heavy on the ground and the frost so thick you could cut it with a knife, when they banished Roger Williams from the Bay Colony. There was some talk of shipping him back to England, but he got wind of that and escaped in time. Off he went, then, over the snows to Narragansett Bay, fifty miles to the south. Let him tell it:

> I was driven from my chamber to a winter's flight, exposed to the miseries, poverties, wants, debts, hardships of sea and land. . . . I was sorely tossed for fourteen weeks in a bitter winter season, not knowing what bread and bed did mean.

And he added words that mean as much today as the day he wrote them:

> Monstrous that God's children should persecute God's children, and that they that hope to live together eternally with Christ in the heavens should not suffer each other to live in this common air together.

A pleasant land, this Narragansett Bay country, that is now Rhode Island. A hundred green islands dot the sparkling blue waters, long sandy beaches invite you to play and to swim, and fir trees crowd down almost to the water's edge. If you go there today you will see a thousand white sailboats rocking up and down in the waves, and the shores lined with houses as thick together as the trees.

But when Roger Williams and a handful of his friends fled across the frozen snow to the bay there was nothing there at all—nothing but a few Indian huts and a straggling of Narragansett Indians.

Mr. Williams didn't mind that. He was out of the Massachusetts Bay Colony and safe, and besides he liked the Indians. Now he could set up his own colony and his own government. Pretty soon he was joined by others from Salem, and even from Boston—Mistress Anne Hutchinson, for example, and her husband and children and friends. She was just as bold as Mr. Williams himself. And boldness was worse in a woman than in a man, so she too was banished by the rulers of the Bay Colony. When she asked why, the governor replied, "Say no more, the Court knows wherefore and is satisfied." That wasn't much of an answer.

So Roger Williams and Anne Hutchinson and their friends set up the colony of Rhode Island—the smallest of all the colonies, but by no means the least important. Three things about that colony made it something special in the history of the world. The first was that Roger Williams treated the Indians justly. He made peace with them, bought their land from them at a fair price, and stayed friends with them. The second was that Mr. Williams arranged for the settlers to govern themselves—all of them, not just the members of a church. But it was the third thing that was the most important of all. Roger Williams not only believed in freedom of religion for himself, he believed in it for others too. He promised that everybody who settled in his colony of Rhode Island would be allowed to worship just as he pleased. . . . Really everybody, not just those who promised not to make trouble and who agreed with Mr. Willams.

And over the years everybody *did* come—other Baptists

and Seekers like Roger Williams, Quakers who were hunted out of the Bay Colony, Jews who built the first American synagogue in Williams' colony. And the example that Rhode Island set—freedom for all to worship as they pleased—was like a flame that grew brighter and brighter with the passing years and finally lit up the whole of the American colonies.

Roger Williams was just getting his colony in Rhode Island started when William Penn was born. And William Penn got his colony of Pennsylvania under way while Roger Williams was still alive to see it.

The two men were not really very much alike, but we remember them for the same things. Both were Englishmen who planted colonies in America. Both believed in religious freedom—and, what is more, practiced it.

Admiral William Penn was a great swell. He lived in a splendid house north of London, he owned farms in England and Ireland, he had been knighted by a grateful King. And—this turned out to be important—he was rich enough to lend money to the King. You didn't think Kings ever needed money, did you? In those days they did. They spent so much money they were always poor. That didn't mean that they had to go without lunch, or sell the family silver, or anything; it just meant that they had to raise more money, somehow or other. Like borrowing it from Admiral Penn.

Admiral Penn had a son, and he named him William too. A fine boy he was, handsome, clever, high-spirited; how proud the admiral was of his son, a chip off the old block, he thought. Young William was already a gentleman born; now his father sent him to Oxford to learn to be a scholar, and to France to learn something of the great world of society, and after that a little law, and then a tour with the royal navy and a bit of soldiering, too, just for good measure. Then he was taught to manage some of the family farms, and in the winter he could be up in London with the King. What a glittering life for a young man—country houses and city houses and titles and money, and beautiful brocade and velvet suits and a sword hanging from his belt, and the King to talk to!

Yes, but it didn't work out that way at all.

For young William had a mind of his own. He loved and respected his father, and he tried his best to be a dutiful son. But he couldn't go along with his father's ideas of high society and clanking swords and all the rest of it. No country estates for him, no fox hunting, no uniforms, no brocades and velvets, no kings or lords or ladies. He had tried all that when he was young, but now he had found another life, sweeter by far than the life of the soldier or the courtier. He had become a Quaker.

In the 1600s England was bursting with new religious ideas. England had become *Protestant*, and when you start *protesting* it is hard to stop. One little group after another found its own religion and formed its own society. There were the Puritans who wanted to purify things, and the Separatists who wanted to separate from the existing church, and the Come-outers who wanted to come out of the old society, and the Seekers who were looking for new truth. And there were the Friends. People called them Quakers, because they quaked and trembled—before God.

Quakers believed that religion was a private matter. It was an inner light that guided you. Religion didn't depend on churches or preachers, they said, and it didn't depend on the King or on the government. For if the King could control religious faith, that would "enthrone man as King over conscience." And of course only God was King over the conscience of man.

Quakers wouldn't take oaths—they wouldn't *swear* to anything. That, they thought, was all wrong: after all, truth was truth, and it didn't become more true just because you swore to it.

Quakers wouldn't take off their hats for men—not even for judges or kings. Only for God.

They thought all show was wrong—all fancy dress, all luxury and waste, all parties and dances and balls. They dressed in plain gray and brown, and lived as gray and brown as they could.

They thought war was wrong—very, very wrong—and they would have no part in fighting.

They loved peace and quiet and simplicity; they loved truth and justice.

You would think all that was harmless enough, wouldn't you? But really it was very dangerous. At least that's what the King and the judges and the bishops all thought. Very dangerous, indeed!

Suppose everyone had his own religion! What would happen to the Church?

Suppose no one would fight? How would the King fight wars and win them?

Suppose nobody would dress up or give parties! Think how dull life would be.

And what was all this about keeping your hat on in the presence of the King! No King could be expected to stand for that.

So down with the Quakers. What they were preaching was dangerous. Send them all to jail. If they wanted peace and quiet they could have their fill of it there—and even keep their hats on, if they wanted!

To jail even with young William Penn. To be sure he was the son of a famous father, but even that wouldn't help him now. Teach him a lesson—teach all these fine young fellows a lesson!

That was a hard blow for the old admiral, you may be sure. The admiral had fought for his King on the high seas, and now his son said all that was wrong. The admiral had fine houses and fine horses and fine silver and linen and silks, and now his son said all must live simply, and he wouldn't use any of these possessions. The admiral was a friend of the King, and now his son wouldn't even take his hat off to the King. The admiral had always been upright and respectable, and now his son was thrown into jail just like a criminal!

So there they were, two good men, the father weeping for his son, and the son weeping for his father, and nothing to do about it.

After a while poor old Admiral Penn died, grieving to the last over his son.

And what of young William Penn—now no longer so young? He went his way, more of a Quaker every day. Sometimes he was in jail, and sometimes he was out of jail, but he was always preaching his religion, or writing books about it, or helping his less fortunate Quaker friends out of trouble. And now, like the Pilgrims, he looked across the sea to the New World that had been opened up, to America. If Quakers couldn't worship in peace in England, perhaps they would be allowed to worship in peace in America.

Now William Penn, and the Quakers, had a stroke of good fortune.

King Charles II owed Admiral Penn a great deal of money. And of course, now that the old admiral was dead, the King owed it to his son William. But kings don't like to pay back money any more than other people. And as for William—he didn't need the money. What would *he* do with money, when all he wanted was the simple life? But then he had a brilliant idea; even King Charles thought it was a brilliant idea. Let the King give Mr. Penn land in America instead of money. That wouldn't cost him a penny, and William Penn would have the land for his Quakers.

So King Charles made over an enormous area of land right in the middle of his American colonies—a beautiful country, watered by rivers with melodious Indian names like Susquehanna and Allegheny and Juniata, and covered with dense forests. He called it Pennsylvania, which is Latin for "Penn's woods."

Pennsylvania! North from Chesapeake Bay to New York, west from the Delaware across the great Allegheny Mountains, almost to Lake Erie. What a princely domain! It was as big as England, and bigger than many European states. Imagine giving away England! Imagine giving away Holland or Denmark!

Pennsylvania for the Quakers. What a wonderful way to pay a debt.

Already William Penn was busy planning his new commonwealth. It was to be a model state—a state based on the Quaker ideas of justice and truth and love. It was to be a refuge for Quakers, but not just for Quakers. It was to be open to all men and women of all countries and all faiths. It was to be a country where everyone would live in peace with everyone else, even with the Indians. It was to be a "Holy Experiment."

And that's just what it was, too. Penn himself sailed over to his colony in 1682 with twenty-two ships all filled with eager colonists. "The air," he wrote, "is sweet and good, the land fertile, and springs many and pleasant." And every year more boats plowed through the waters of the Atlantic and up the Delaware River to the bright new town which Penn had laid out and named Philadelphia, which means "City of Brotherly Love." On they came, from England, from Scotland, from Wales, from Holland, from Germany, flooding into this beautiful country where the air was sweet and good because it was the air of peace, and where the springs were pleasant because all alike could drink from them, of whatever race, whatever tongue, whatever faith.

Roger Williams and William Penn were very great men.

But the man who did most for freedom of religion was probably Thomas Jefferson of Virginia.

Sometimes when you read history you come across men who are monsters of wickedness. You come across conquerors like the Spaniard Francisco Pizarro, who killed off almost all the Indians in Peru. You come across kings like Charles IX of France, who gave the order for the Massacre of St. Bartholomew, in which thirty or forty thousand unoffending Protestants were killed. You come across dictators like Hitler, who sent six million men and women to their death because they were Jewish. It makes you wonder if the human race is worth reading about.

Then you come to a man like Thomas Jefferson, and you know that it is.

If you read about Thomas Jefferson in a novel you wouldn't believe in him. Nobody, you would say, nobody could be that good and that wise and that great, all at once. And you would almost be right.

If Thomas Jefferson weren't true, he would be too good to be true.

He was tall and handsome, he was freckled and smiling, and his blue eyes looked out from under a mop of red hair; even now after almost two hundred years it makes you feel good just to look at a picture of him. He was strong and quick, he could find his way through the forest like an Indian, and he could ride his horse like a cavalier.

He was a farmer. So were most Americans of his day. But he was probably the best farmer in Virginia, and maybe in all America. He knew everything there was to know about farming. He experimented with new crops, planted new kinds of vines, brought in new kinds of sheep, tried new kinds of plowing and fertilizing. He made his farm look like a garden, and he made his garden look like a beautiful painting.

He was an architect, and in time he came to be the best architect in America. He built a beautiful house on top of a mountain in the Blue Ridge, and called it Monticello, or "Little Mountain." You can still see it there, one of the loveliest houses ever built. He built the University of Virginia, too, first planning every detail, sitting there in Monticello and watching it through a telescope to make sure that it was all done right.

He was a scholar. He collected books on all subjects and in all languages; and he didn't just collect them, he read them and used them. In the end he had the best library in all America and he gave most of it to start the Library of Congress in Washington, which is today the greatest library in the world.

He was a scientist; he knew all about chemistry and physics, botany and biology, geography and geology, and he carried on experiments in the laboratory he had built for himself at Monticello. Most of the great scientific societies in America and Europe were proud to have him as a member, and most of the great scientists were his friends.

He was an inventor. He couldn't see anything without trying to improve it. He invented a plow so good that all Europe sang its praises. He invented doors that folded to open and unfolded to close—you can see them on telephone booths today. He invented a special writing machine that would make a copy of his letters as he wrote them, and beds that pulled up to the ceiling, and all sorts of things.

He was a lawyer. When he was young he practiced law in the courts and won most of his cases. After a while he stopped practicing law and instead wrote laws—a good many of the laws of his own state of Virginia.

He was a musician. He fiddled on his violin; he imported workingmen from Italy just so they could play for him; he said music was the dearest thing in his life.

He was an educator. He planned a whole new school system for Virginia and then he planned one for all the new states that were going to come into the Union—Ohio and Indiana and Illinois and the others. He planned the University of Virginia, and built it, and laid out the grounds, and selected the library and appointed the professors and picked the students. It was Mr. Jefferson's university.

He was a literary man. He wrote hundreds of important papers and thousands of letters, and they are probably the most interesting letters ever written in America. Now, more than two hundred years after he was born, we are still reading his letters just as if they were written to us.

But we have hardly even begun on Thomas Jefferson. Look at all the things we have left out:

He wrote the Declaration of Independence. He wrote it when he was thirty-three years old. You may not think that is so remarkable, but your father and mother will; after all, who else ever wrote a Declaration of Independence at thirty-three? Or at any other age, for that matter?

He drew up the plans for the government of the vast country west of the Allegheny Mountains—that is, for the states where most of you now live.

He was President Washington's Secretary of State.

He founded the Democratic party—the first and the oldest political party in the world.

He was Vice-President of the United States.

He was President of the United States for eight years—and he could have gone on being President for the rest of his life had he wanted.

He doubled the size of the United States by buying all the land between the Mississippi River and the Rocky Mountains. Then he sent Lewis and Clark across the Rocky Mountains and on to the Pacific Ocean just so we could keep our hand in all that territory too.

He lived to be the Grand Old Man of American politics—of American life for that matter—the most beloved man in the country.

He died on the Fourth of July 1826, exactly fifty years after the signing of the Declaration of Independence!

A great American judge, Oliver Wendell Holmes, once said, "Life is not doing a sum, life is painting a picture."

It wasn't just the sums that Jefferson did that were important, though he did more sums than anybody else who ever lived in America. It was the picture he painted that was important.

If you study the picture of life that Thomas Jefferson painted—and a big picture it is, covering sixty years of work—if you study it you will see that it is bathed in sunlight.

As Thomas Jefferson looked out on his world he was filled with wonder and excitement and happiness and hope.

He looked at nature and he found it beautiful.

He looked at his fellow men and he found them good and kind and intelligent.

He looked up to the heavens and all their wonders, and he saw that God had created a marvelous universe, and he knew that man was one of the marvels of the universe.

"Providence," he said in his Inaugural Address, "delights in the happiness of man here, and his greater happiness hereafter."

Men were meant to be happy, to be good, and to be wise. Men were meant to master themselves, and the world that they lived in.

But there was one stern condition for all this. It was what went along with life and happiness in the Declaration of Independence. Remember? It was *liberty*.

Men would be happy when they were free.

Men would be good when they were free.

Men would be wise when they were free.

Men would master themselves and their world, but only when they were free.

To Thomas Jefferson freedom was a religion. He gave his life to fighting for freedom and to fighting against tyranny.

"I have sworn upon the altar of God eternal hostility against every form of tyranny over the mind of man," he said. And again:

"Rebellion to tyrants is obedience to God." He took that for his motto.

Freedom. Freedom from slavery. Freedom from tyranny. Freedom from superstition. Freedom from ignorance. Freedom of thought, of speech, of the press. Freedom of religion.

So now we come to this chapter of Thomas Jefferson's life—the chapter that tells what he did for freedom of religion.

When Jefferson wrote the Declaration of Independence he meant that America should be independent all the way. Independent in government. Independent in army and in navy. Independent in trade and commerce, independent in land, independent in schools. And independent in churches and religion.

In England, of course, there was just one church—just one that the government recognized and supported. That was called the Church of England. And the English had brought the Church of England over to America and set it up in some of the colonies—among them in Jefferson's colony of Virginia. They had made it *the* Church—the only church where you could get properly christened and properly buried. According to them, you weren't even sure of your name unless it had been given to you in the Church of England, and you weren't at all sure of going to heaven unless you had been buried from the Church of England!

Independence meant that Americans would cut loose from the Church of England just as they cut loose from England herself.

All very well to cut loose from England—but surely not from the Church! Surely you do not suggest that Virginia shouldn't have any church at all!

But that is just what Thomas Jefferson did suggest; that

*Virginia* was not to have any church at all—*Virginia,* mind you. Let Virginians have all the churches they wanted. Let every man in America have his own church. Let every church stand on its own foundations—Baptist, Presbyterian, Episcopal, Quaker, and all the others. But let them all be independent, just like the United States. No Virginia church, no United States church.

No government has the right to *make* anybody support a church or to put one before others. That is the way Jefferson reasoned. That is the way his young friend James Madison reasoned too—Madison who worked with Jefferson all his life, half like a brother, half like a son, and who succeeded him in the White House.

It was while he was governor of Virginia that Jefferson wrote the Bill for Religious Freedom in Virginia. But he couldn't get it passed at once. There were months and years of argument. Wouldn't this destroy all religion? Wouldn't it upset everything? Wouldn't it plunge Virginia into wickedness and ungodliness?

Of course not, said Jefferson. His bill wouldn't hurt religion; it would help religion. It would make the churches stand on their own feet. It would make religion a matter of free choice.

Finally Jefferson won out, Jefferson and his friend Madison. In 1786 his Bill for Religious Freedom became law.

It started off with a grand line: "Whereas . . . God hath created the mind free."

And it closed with a great line, too: "Truth is great and will prevail, if left to herself."

Jefferson was in France when his Bill for Religious Freedom finally passed. How he rejoiced. And how all Europe rejoiced. Free men everywhere, in England and France, Germany and Italy, hailed this law as one of the great landmarks in the history of freedom.

So it was, too. Yet actually it was limited to the little state of Virginia.

But look ahead just three years and see what is happening.

Now Americans had written a new Constitution, and adopted it, and set up a new government. Now George Washington was President of the United States. Now Jefferson was back from France as his Secretary of State, and now, too, his friend James Madison was in the new Congress, writing the new laws.

He wasn't much to look at, "Jemmy" Madison, a little man not much taller than most of you, modest and mild and with a voice so low you could hardly hear him when he talked. The littlest man in Congress, but the biggest one, too. . . . The lowest voice—and the voice that comes to us most clearly down through all these years.

No sooner had Washington taken the oath as President, and the Congress settled down to work, than up stood Mr. Madison. He had a long paper in his hand, and he started to read it. It was a Bill of Rights—a list of all the rights that belonged to the American people, and that Congress would have to protect and preserve. And the very first one of them was this:

> "Congress shall make no law respecting an establishment of religion, or prohibiting the free exercise thereof."

There you are. It was the same thing as the Virginia law for religious freedom, only now it was national. It said: hands off religion, hands off the church. Religion is a matter between man and God, and not a matter for the state to meddle with.

And that's the way it stands in our Constitution today.

So what began with the Pilgrims over in Holland, and with Roger Williams escaping across the snows to Narragansett Bay, ended up with Jefferson's bill in Virginia and with Madison's amendment to the Constitution. What began as an idea that was hunted from country to country ended up as the great basic idea of a great nation.

And not of one nation alone. For this idea—that every man has a *right* to worship as he will, and that the state must keep hands off—has spread from country to country and from continent to continent, and has become one of the great ideas of the human race.

# FREEDOM FROM SLAVERY

CAUTION!!
COLORED PEOPLE
WATCHMEN
UNCLE TOMS
SALE
THIS DAY

Imagine owning somebody!

Imagine being owned by somebody!

You can't imagine it—not really. You can read *Uncle Tom's Cabin,* and feel sorry for poor old Uncle Tom, or for Eliza crossing the frozen Ohio River with her baby in her arms, but you can't really know what it is like to be a slave.

Yet millions and millions of men and women have been slaves—and so have boys and girls, too, for that matter—even here in America. If you are a Negro some of your forebears were slaves, and not too far back, either, for it is only one hundred years ago that the United States put an end to slavery.

Slavery is very old. It is as old as the first civilizations in Babylonia and Assyria. In some ways it is older even than freedom, for men were slaves before men had truly learned to be free.

Remember how Joseph and his brethren were sold into slavery in Egypt?

Remember how the ancient Greeks made slaves of those they captured in war? Why, one general—he was named Nicias—owned a thousand slaves!

Remember how the Romans made slaves of Christians, and of most of the other people they captured in their constant wars?

All of these slaves were white men and women. But in modern times it is mostly Negroes and Indians who have been made slaves.

Slavery in America started when Christopher Columbus discovered the islands of the Caribbean and planted the Spanish flag on them. Almost the first thing the Spanish conquerors did was to make slaves of the gentle Carib Indians—the ones who gave us the name Caribbean—and then drove them to the hopeless task of finding gold and silver, hopeless because there was no gold and silver. . . . The poor Carib Indians couldn't live under slavery. Many of them were killed off by their brutal conquerors, others languished away and died. Then the Spaniards committed one of the great crimes of history. They kidnaped Negroes from Africa and shipped them over to the Caribbean islands to be slaves.

That is the way Negro slavery was first brought to America.

One hot day in 1619 a Dutch ship sailed into the waters of Chesapeake Bay and up the James River to the tiny settlement of Jamestown, the very first English settlement in America. That ship carried just about the worst cargo that any ship ever brought to American shores.

It carried a cargo of Negro slaves.

Of course you can't really blame the Dutch ship for that. If it hadn't been that ship it would have been another one. In fact four years later an English ship named the

*Treasurer* came sailing in with another cargo of Negro slaves.

Actually nobody seemed to mind very much. Everybody knew about slavery, and almost everybody took it pretty much for granted. It was convenient to have Negroes who could work in the tobacco fields under the broiling sun, or who were strong enough to cut down the trees that stood in the fields, and haul them away. It was convenient to have Negro women who could cook dinners over the hot fires, and Negro children to do the chores around the farm.

Convenient, that is, for the white people who owned them. Not so convenient perhaps for the Negro slaves. But then nobody asked them, and if they had, the poor Negroes would not have understood what they were talking about.

So gradually more and more slaves were brought to America. The slave traders who brought them made a fortune. The slave dealers who sold them made a fortune. The farmers and planters who bought them didn't make all that much money, but they did pretty well for themselves, having someone to do all the hard work. Everybody seemed to profit from slavery—except the slaves. Nobody cared whether they profited or not.

So slavery grew and slavery spread. Every year thousands of Negroes were brought in from Africa, or from the islands of the West Indies, to do the hard work—to raise tobacco in Virginia, to make turpentine in the woods of North Carolina, to cultivate the rice fields of South Carolina, to cut the sugar cane of Louisiana. And one day, not long after the United States became a nation, a young man named Eli Whitney who was visiting down in Georgia figured out a clever way to take the hundreds of little seeds out of cotton bolls and thus make it possible to spin the cotton into cloth. Soon everybody was raising cotton. And of course everybody needed slaves for that too.

Didn't it worry the white masters to own Negro slaves? Didn't they ever ask themselves why God should have made white people to be masters and black people to be slaves?

Didn't they read in their Bible that men should do unto others as they would have others do unto them?

Didn't they read the Declaration of Independence which said that "all men are created equal?"

Didn't they read the Bill of Rights? And did they think it was meant only for them—freedom of religion, freedom of speech, fair trial, equal treatment before the law, and all the rest of it—just for white people?

The answer is that most of them never thought of these things at all.

Almost everybody in the South simply took slavery for granted, just as you take for granted that you have enough to eat, even though most of the people of the world do not have enough to eat; or just as you take for granted that you go to school, even though most of the boys and girls of the world don't have any school to go to.

Yes, the white people of the South took slavery for granted. What's more, they came to think that slavery was really a very good thing. It was a good thing for them, and it was even a good thing for the slaves.

It took them out of Africa and civilized them.

It made Christians of them, and thus saved their souls.

It took care of them, fed them, clothed them, sheltered them, and nursed them in childhood and in old age.

What a wonderful institution!

It is surprising that all the white people didn't blacken their faces and become slaves themselves, it was such a wonderful institution!

That's just what Abraham Lincoln once said. "Whenever I hear anyone arguing for slavery, I feel a strong impulse to see it tried on him."

Most masters treated their slaves kindly. After all, that was not only the right thing to do, it was the sensible thing to do, for slaves (like everybody else) worked better when they were treated right. But not everybody is kind, and not everybody is sensible. There were always some slaveowners who were in a great hurry to get rich and who drove their poor slaves as hard as they could.

Even at its best, slavery was hard. It meant long hours of work under the hot sun, and nothing to look forward to even—nothing but slavery all your life. And at its worst? . . . Well, then it meant long hours of work, too, and such food as your master gave you, and such rags as he let you wear, and such cabins as he built for you. It meant a whipping if you didn't work as hard as he thought you should, or if you answered back, or if you ran away—worse than a whipping, then, the bloodhounds out after you and the red-hot branding iron on your cheek if they caught you. It meant husbands sold away from wives and wives sold away from husbands, and mothers and children torn apart.

Some white people in the South—even some of the slaveowners themselves—saw all this. They saw that slavery was wrong, that it was wrong for whites and blacks alike. Thomas Jefferson, for instance: "I tremble for my country when I reflect that God is just," he wrote. And when he drew up a plan of government for the new states in the West he wrote in a provision that there should be no slavery in all that country. The Quakers, too, both north and south, thought that slavery was hateful, and fought it with all their might.

But how do you fight slavery?

Do you just sit back and wait for it to die out by itself?

That was all very well in Massachusetts or in New York.

There it *did* die out by itself—and in other Northern states as well. It wasn't that Yankees and Yorkers were so good. They were no better than anybody else. It was rather that slavery simply didn't work well in their country. It didn't pay to use slaves on the rocky farms of New England. It didn't pay to use slaves in the factories of New York or Pennsylvania. So one by one the states of the North set their slaves free—there weren't many of them, after all—until in the end there were no more slaves north of Maryland or of the Ohio River.

But that didn't mean that the folks up north were going to *fight* slavery. Nothing was further from their minds. That was asking for trouble.

After all, if Yankees didn't want slavery that was *their* business.

And if Southerners did want slavery, that was *their* business.

Nobody asked what the slaves wanted—their business was to be slaves.

Anybody who stirred up the slavery question was a troublemaker. And you know what happens to troublemakers!

Elijah Lovejoy stirred up trouble with his newspaper in Alton, Illinois, and they shot him dead.

When Prudence Crandall stirred up trouble in Connecticut by letting a little Negro girl come to her school, they destroyed the school—and Miss Crandall's home too.

When Quakers stirred up trouble in Philadelphia by holding a meeting against slavery in the new Pennsylvania Hall, they burned down the hall.

When the headmaster of Noyes Academy up in New Hampshire stirred up trouble by admitting some Negro pupils to his school, the townspeople hitched a hundred oxen to the steeple of his school and pulled it down.

When Thomas Garrett of Wilmington, Delaware, stirred

up trouble by helping Negroes escape from slavery, they clapped him in jail and fined him ten thousand dollars.

And when William Lloyd Garrison stirred up trouble with his *Liberator* newspaper, they put a rope around his neck and tried to hang him.

William Lloyd Garrison was born to trouble as Roger Williams was born to religion.

He had known trouble all his life. When he was a little boy his father had run away from wife and children, and his mother had gone to work to support them all. When he was nine years old he went to work himself—first for a shoemaker, then in a carpenter's shop, then as printer's "devil," which is what an apprentice in a printing shop was called.

So far nothing very special about Garrison. After all, lots of boys are poor and go to work.

No, William Lloyd Garrison didn't become interesting until he got interested in something himself. And what he got interested in was slavery.

Interested! That isn't quite the word. He got slavery on the brain. He spent all his waking hours thinking about slavery, and when he went to sleep he dreamed about slavery. He buttonholed everybody he saw and talked about slavery, so that when his friends saw him coming they hurried over to the other side of the street or ducked into some shop. . . . It was like an electric current that was never turned off; it was like a fire that burned and burned, and smoked and smoked.

Garrison talked about slavery, he made speeches about it, he wrote about it. He said the same thing over and over: slavery was against nature, slavery was against Christianity, slavery was a sin and slaveholders were all sinners.

In 1831 he founded his own newspaper to fight slavery—

remember? He called it the *Liberator,* and the name tells you how Garrison planned to fight slavery. He planned to liberate the slaves.

> I determined [he said] to lift up the standard of freedom in the eyes of the nation, within sight of Bunker Hill and in the birthplace of liberty. My standard is now unfurled, and long may it float, till every bondman be set free.

What a tiresome young man, pounding away on this one note, over and over, day in and day out, like a whippoorwill. But "I will be heard" he said, and he was heard. They tried to stop his paper, but instead it caught on and was read more widely every year. They tried to stop him too—they put him in jail and tried to lynch him but all in vain. You could no more stop William Lloyd Garrison than you could stop thunder and lightning.

He started a society to fight slavery—the American Antislavery Society, he called it. How ridiculous. Nobody would join such a society, anyway nobody but a lot of old women. . . . But within ten years a quarter of a million people had joined anti-slavery societies.

That was one way to fight slavery—by writing with such fire that the words burned right through the newspaper and into the minds and hearts of those who read them.

Theodore Parker had another way to fight slavery.

He, too, was a Massachusetts boy, born in the little town of Lexington. It was his grandfather, Captain Parker, who had stood on Lexington Common early on the morning of the nineteenth of April 1775 and fired the first shots of the Revolutionary War.

Theodore Parker always kept his grandfather's gun hanging on the wall above the fireplace in his study.

An odd place for a gun—in a minister's study.

For Theodore Parker was a preacher. He was not only *a* preacher; he was *the* Great American Preacher, with capital letters. That's what he was called, even in his lifetime. He had the largest parish in Boston; he stood in his pulpit in the Music Hall every Sunday morning and preached to two thousand men and women who hung on every word he said—every word of his prayers and every word of his sermons.

But that isn't why he was called The Great American Preacher. It was because he took the whole nation for his parish, and preached to the whole nation. Back and forth he went, now in New York, now in Wisconsin, now up in Maine, now in Pennsylvania, sitting in cold railway cars, sleeping in strange hotel rooms, preaching in crowded halls and churches: everybody in America, it seemed, wanted to hear him. Well—not quite everybody; let us say everybody who hated slavery wanted to hear him. And those who couldn't hear him hurried out to buy his sermons as soon as they were printed, and then passed them around for all their neighbors to read.

Out in Illinois a young lawyer named Abraham Lincoln read his sermons. "Theodore Parker is my kind of Christian," he said. One thing that the Reverend Mr. Parker wrote Lincoln remembered all his life: "Democracy is self-government over all the people, for all the people, by all the people."

What was it about Theodore Parker that made him the best loved, and the best hated, preacher in America?

It was partly the kind of person he was; it was partly what he stood for and what he did.

He was a farmer boy, and there was always something of the country about him. He was simple and staunch and sincere; no show, no pretense. He was terribly in earnest. In everything he said and did you could tell that he was generous and just.

He couldn't stand injustice, and he fought it all his life.

He fought for justice for workingmen in shops and factories.

He fought for justice for women who were denied the rights of men.

He fought for justice for little children who had to work instead of going to school.

He fought for justice for the poor, the helpless, and the criminal—he called them "the dangerous and perishing classes" of society.

He fought for justice for the slave.

How he fought! One mighty sermon after another from that pulpit in the Music Hall, listing the wrongs of slavery and calling on Christians to put an end to it. Presidents read the sermons, and senators, and governors, and judges: some of them loved Mr. Parker, some of them were afraid of him, but all of them respected him and listened to him when he spoke.

But that wasn't all, the sermons and the lectures and the letters. The grandson of Captain Parker wasn't content with that. Every runaway slave who came to Boston headed for Theodore Parker's house, there in Exeter Place. They were fearful and hopeless, many of them, but courage streamed out of Parker like light out of the sun. They knew that he would protect them and that he would somehow hurry them on to Canada where they would be safe. And he did. Whenever the slaveholders came to Boston looking for their runaway slaves, Mr. Parker would print a big poster and put it up all over town:

CAUTION!!!
COLORED PEOPLE OF
BOSTON
KIDNAPPERS AND
SLAVE CATCHERS
PEOPLE OF
BOSTON
RALLY TO FREEDOM!

And rally they did, too, with the Reverend Mr. Parker at their head. Imagine a minister organizing a vigilante committee to protect Negroes! Imagine a minister defying the judges and the governors and the soldiers in order to save Negro slaves.

You couldn't scare Mr. Parker.

Once at a big meeting in New York the speaker said, "If Mr. Parker were here I would charge him with treason." "Oh, you would, would you?" said Mr. Parker, who was up in the gallery. "Here I am, go ahead and charge me and let me answer you."

Once he was arrested for helping a slave escape. "Wonderful," he said, "just let them bring me to trial." He wrote a three-hundred-page defense, and the judge was so staggered that he didn't dare bring Parker to trial, but called the whole thing off.

Theodore Parker was a great scholar, one of the greatest in the land. He was a preacher who loved peace. But more than anything else he loved freedom. He gave his life to preaching freedom for the slave.

That was another way to fight slavery.

There was a third way, the simplest of all.

That was to help the slave run away from slavery—run away to the North, to Canada, to freedom.

It meant getting across the magic line that separated slavery from freedom.

Look at the map and you can trace that line. It ran along the border of Pennsylvania, and along the Ohio River all the way to where it flows into the Mississippi. On one side was slavery, on the other side was freedom. Only a thin line, but two worlds almost as different as the world of life and of death.

How do you cross from one world to another—if you are a slave?

Well, mostly you don't. You just live and die a slave.

But some did. Some managed to run away and make their way across that line and win their freedom.

But oh, it was hard. It was harder than breaking out of jail.

Remember, a slave had no education. He couldn't read. He certainly couldn't read a map. He knew no more about roads and rivers and woods and mountains than you know about the geography of the moon. Maybe less. How was he to find his way through a strange country for one or two hundred miles?

Remember, too, a slave had no rights. Certainly he had no right to be out by himself wandering through the countryside, or walking along the roads or the streets of a town. He had no right to be out at night at all—and since that was the only time he could be out, he had to keep in hiding all the time.

And remember, if a slave ran away every man's hand was against him, and everybody was after him.

His master would put a notice in all the papers:

WANTED

GEORGE

A RUNAWAY SLAVE.

HE IS 24 YEARS OLD, LIGHT COLORED AND TALL. HE HAS ONLY FOUR FINGERS ON HIS LEFT HAND. WHEN LAST SEEN HE WAS DRESSED IN BLUE PANTALOONS AND A BLUE SHIRT

REWARD!!!

Everybody would be on the lookout for him. Everybody would be eager to catch him and send him back to his master to be branded on the cheek with the letter R for Runaway. Or worse yet the bloodhounds would be out after him, tracking him down in the woods or the swamp.

Only by running through a flowing stream could he throw them off the scent.

How did a slave ever reach freedom? Yet thousands of them did. Somehow they managed to follow the North Star to Pennsylvania or Ohio or Indiana, and to freedom.

Southerners said that slaves were happy as the day is long. Yet thousands of them braved death to run away to freedom, but not one of them ever went the other way, from freedom to slavery. Not one.

If you asked a runaway slave how he managed to escape he would tell you that he took the Underground Railroad.

You've probably heard of the *Underground* in London. That's what they call their subway, railroad cars running on tracks in a network of underground tunnels.

The original Underground Railroad goes back to the 1830s—just when the first real railroads were being built in England and America. It didn't have any real tracks, or any real engines or cars, or any real stations. And it certainly didn't run underground.

All the same, that was a good name for it: the Underground Railroad.

Its tracks were dusty country roads that stretched from the Ohio River northward toward the Great Lakes and Canada, or from Maryland into Pennsylvania and New York—and Canada. Its engines were horses and its cars were ordinary wagons. Its stations were farmhouses and barns scattered about the countryside, known only to those who worked for the Railroad. Its engineers and conductors were courageous men and women who were willing to risk their lives to rescue the slaves. And its passengers were slaves.

How did it work?

Well, look at Levi Coffin, who helped make it work for twenty-five years.

He was born in North Carolina—that was slave country

of course. But he was a Quaker, and Quakers, you will remember, didn't hold with slavery. So, like many other Quakers, Levi decided to go north, to get away from slavery. And in 1826, when President Adams was in the White House, he moved across the Ohio River to a little town in Indiana called Newport.

His daytime work was running a store, and he ran it well and made money and was respected by everyone in his part of the state. His nighttime work was running a station on the Underground Railroad.

Here's how it worked:

Picture to yourself a dark night, long past midnight, the little town of Newport fast asleep. A hay wagon crunches along the country road and pulls up at Levi Coffin's barn —it's not safe to go to the front door, someone might see you. . . . There is a soft rat-tat-tat on the door, or maybe some gravel thrown against the windowpanes. Levi and his wife wake up instantly—they are used to this—or maybe they have been warned, and are sitting up in the dark waiting. A whispered password then—"two bales of cotton" perhaps, or "two barrels of apples"—and the door is opened. Two frightened Negroes tumble out of the back of the wagon, brushing the hay out of their hair, their eyes big with fear. "Come along," says Levi, and takes them by the hand, and the door closes, and the blinds are drawn, and the only light comes from a log smoldering in the fireplace.

First a bowl of hot soup, for it can be cold crossing the Ohio, even in the summer. Then quickly up the stairs to the attic, or out to the barn, and under the hay. Then the wagon will drive off to a nearby farm, for if it is standing there in the morning the neighbors will be curious—and the slave catchers too.

For next day the slave catchers will be in town, looking for the runaways. But they won't know where to look, and no one will tell them. In a few days the coast is clear; then Levi Coffin will hitch up his carriage and put his two runaways in the back and cover them over with parcels of merchandise, and off he will go, eight or ten miles into the country to the next station on the Underground Railroad. And so on—and on—and on, from station to station, following the North Star, to freedom.

Sometimes it was easy enough, especially in the summer. Sometimes in the winter it was touch and go. Then the snow would show the pursuers the tracks of the wagon wheels; then the poor runaways would arrive so frozen that they couldn't walk, and Levi would have to keep them hidden away in his warehouse or his barn for weeks until they were well enough to go on.

One of the runaways who came to Levi Coffin one winter night was named Eliza Harris. Running through the night with her pursuers hot on her trail, and a baby in her arms, she had crossed the Ohio River on the ice and found her way to Levi Coffin's house. Mr. Coffin told that story to a preacher's wife named Harriet Beecher Stowe, in nearby Cincinnati. And Harriet Beecher Stowe told it to the whole world in one of the most exciting books ever written: *Uncle Tom's Cabin.*

When Abraham Lincoln met Harriet Beecher Stowe at the White House he said to her, "So this is the little woman who made the Civil War."

For twenty-five years Levi Coffin ran his station on the Underground Railroad, and in all that time he never lost a passenger.

Neither did Harriet Tubman.

If you were asked to name some of the great women of history you would say Joan of Arc . . . and Queen Elizabeth . . . and Florence Nightingale . . . and Eleanor Roosevelt. . . . Certainly you would never say Harriet Tubman. You never even *heard* of her. Scarcely anybody has ever heard of her.

Yet she is one of the great women of history.

She was born a slave, on a Maryland plantation, and given the fancy name of Araminta, which she later changed to plain Harriet. She grew up as strong as any man, able to do a man's work plowing in the fields, or a woman's work cooking in the kitchen. But she could never work hard enough for the brutal overseer who ran the plantation, and once in a fit of temper he threw an iron horseshoe at her and almost killed her. She got well, in time, but after that she was never quite the same: she would fall into a trance, she would go right out of this world and into another world of her imagination where she would see visions and hear voices—just like Joan of Arc.

When Harriet was twenty-five or thirty—it wasn't easy for slaves to keep track of their age—she ran away to nearby Pennsylvania. Good for her! But she wasn't content with that. In one of her visions God told her to go back to Maryland and find her father and mother, her brothers and sisters, and lead them to freedom. And she did.

That was her lifework, to go into the South and guide slaves back across the magic line to the land of freedom. Again and again she made her way deep into Maryland and Virginia—she had a kind of sixth sense about direction, and besides, so she always thought, God guided her. She was clever and shrewd, and could fool almost anyone. Who would ever suspect her of any mischief, this slave woman with a turban wound around her head, and a red bandana at her neck, shuffling along so simple and so innocent? If they *did* she knew how to throw them off the scent. She knew all the hiding places, all the woods and swamps and abandoned barns, in the whole countryside. In the winter months she worked up in Philadelphia, cooking and washing to make money. Then when spring came she was off to the South again. She brought out her parents, driving them herself in an ancient oxcart. She brought out whole families, eight and ten at a time. Sometimes she had to fight to get her slaves away and once—in New York of all places—she rescued a runaway slave from a mob and dragged him through the streets of the town to the riverbank where she pushed him into a boat that carried him off to safety.

Old John Brown—remember him in that poem "Old John Brown, Osawatomie Brown?"—said that Harriet Tubman "was the most man that I ever met with." He ought to know. He was quite a man himself. He was the man who attacked Harper's Ferry—with just a handful of Negroes. He was the man whose body "lies a-mould'ring in the grave—His soul goes marching on."

Harriet Tubman was the Moses of her people, leading them out of the wilderness and into the Promised Land.

Suppose you could save just one person, save one child from drowning, save one old lady from a burning house, give light to one man who was blind. Think how proud and happy you would be: it would be something to remember all your life.

Harriet Tubman saved three hundred lives. She led three hundred slaves across the magic line to freedom.

That's still another way to fight slavery—the way of Levi Coffin and Harriet Tubman.

But none of these ways of fighting slavery really hurt slavery very much. William Lloyd Garrison and Theodore Parker could blast away against slavery, and Levi Coffin and Harriet Tubman could rescue runaways, but slavery was still there. Every year the number of slaves increased —three million in 1850, four million in 1860.

How would it ever end?

In February 1861 Abraham Lincoln was on his way to Washington to be President of the United States. He stopped off at Philadelphia to make a speech about the Declaration of Independence. What did it mean? he asked. It meant, he said, that "weights should be lifted from the shoulders of all men . . . that *all* should have an equal chance."

*All* men? Black as well as white? Slave as well as free? . . . Were *they* to have an equal chance? Why, they hadn't any chance at all.

Yes, all men. Anyhow, that was what Lincoln hoped would happen. He didn't expect it to happen right away, but he expected that it would happen sometime. He had always hated slavery, this Illinois lawyer, hated what it did to the masters as well as to the slaves, to white people as well as to black. But he wasn't like Garrison or Theodore Parker; he didn't think all slaveholders were sinners. After all, he had been born in the South himself, and so had his wife, and he knew slaveowners who were just as good and kind as their Northern cousins. And he wasn't like Levi Coffin, either; he couldn't flout the law to help slaves run away; after all, he was a lawyer and had a duty to uphold the law. Besides, he didn't think it did much good to help an individual slave run away: slavery was still there.

If you are Abraham Lincoln, how do you fight slavery?

"If all earthly power were given me," Lincoln said, "I should not know what to do about slavery." Now he was President of the United States. He didn't have *all* earthly power—nobody ever had that—but he had more power than anyone else.

But as soon as Lincoln became President he had a war on his hands. For now the South had left the Union and set up on her own as the Confederate States of America. She had her own Constitution and her own capital city and her own flag. And now she was fighting for independence.

All along a thousand miles, from the city of Washington west along the Potomac River, across the mountains, westward to the Mississippi River—and even beyond it—out onto the prairie lands of the Far West, soldiers in Union blue are fighting soldiers in Confederate gray.

What are they fighting for, these men and boys in gray?

They are fighting to be independent. They are fighting to keep *their* way of life—a life where white people are allowed to own slaves without anybody criticizing them or trying to take their slaves away from them.

Listen to them as they march along, the Stars and Bars of the Confederate flag fluttering in the breeze:

*In Dixie Land we'll take our stand,*
*To live and die in Dixie . . .*

And what are the men and boys in blue fighting for?

They are fighting for the Union—fighting to keep this land one country instead of two. And they are fighting for freedom. Listen to *them,* as they tramp along the dusty roads of Virginia or Tennessee:

*Yes, we'll rally round the flag, boys,*
*We'll rally once again,*
*Shouting the battle-cry of FREEDOM!*

Could Lincoln make the war for Union a war for freedom too?

Yes, he could, and he did.

Slaves didn't actually fight in the Confederate Army, but they did almost everything else but fight. They took the place of soldiers back on the plantations, and they took the place of soldiers in the army, too, driving the wagons, caring for the horses, building roads, and doing a hundred other useful things.

So slaves were helping to fight a war to break up the Union—and keep slavery! Surely, thought Lincoln, that was reason enough to put an end to slavery.

Besides, by now almost everybody took for granted that slavery would have to go. The English took it for granted; they had got rid of slavery in their West Indian islands thirty years earlier. Most of Europe took it for granted; they hadn't permitted slavery for a hundred years. More and more of the people of the North took it for granted. And more and more of those soldiers in blue, too, marching along shouting the battle cry of freedom.

Lincoln was thinking of all these when he decided that slavery would have to go. But most of all he was thinking of the slaves themselves.

He was thinking of the tens of thousands who had already escaped and gone north: you couldn't round them up and send them back to slavery! He was thinking of the tens of thousands of slaves who had joined the Union armies and were fighting for the Union cause, wearing uniforms that were just as blue as those worn by white soldiers. You couldn't send them back to slavery either. And he was thinking of the millions of men and women and children who were still slaves: it was time they were free. "God," he said, "has decided this question in favor of the slaves."

And on the first day of the new year, 1863, Lincoln published a proclamation saying that hereafter all the slaves in the South would be free.

It was called the Emancipation Proclamation. That is why Lincoln is known as the Great Emancipator.

Of course the proclamation wouldn't mean anything unless the Union won the war.

In the end the Union did win the war.

The Confederates surrendered, there at Appomattox Court House in Virginia, and put away their weapons and folded away their flags, and went home. And slavery was no more.

So it was given to Abraham Lincoln to do one of the great deeds of history.

Who would have thought it?

Who would have thought it of little Abe, growing up in a log cabin out there on the frontier?

Who would have thought it of the boy Abraham, his mother dead, his father a ne'er-do-well?

Who would have thought it of young Lincoln, splitting rails out there on the Illinois prairie, keeping store, poling a raft down the sluggish Illinois River, swapping stories with the boys sitting around the country store?

Who would have thought it of lawyer Lincoln, not much of a lawyer either—no proper schooling, no law training, mostly just his native wit?

Who would have thought it of Congressman Lincoln? Yes, he got to Congress, but for only one term, and then he was sent home by the voters.

Who would have thought it even of President Lincoln? Nobody knew just how *he* got to be President instead of one of the governors or senators or great men of the East.

Who would have thought it of tall, gangling Mr. Lincoln, his face all wrinkles and cheekbone, his hair never rightly combed, his arms too long and his legs too long, his voice all crackly; poor Mr. Lincoln, so plain, so awkward, so countrified that it was hard not to laugh at him when you saw him.

Who would have thought that it would be Abraham Lincoln who would put an end to the greatest wrong in history?

Now all the Negroes in America were free.

No more whipping, no more branding irons. No more separation of mothers and children. No more need to run away.

But freedom is a gradual thing.

It isn't something that happens all at once, and over with—like being asleep and waking up. It is something that happens slowly, over a long time, like growing up. It doesn't come just from the outside, as when you take a blindfold off your eyes and can see. It comes from the inside, too, as when you start *using* your eyes to see things that you never noticed before.

The first step in freedom is of course to strike off the

shackles that make you a slave. But that is only the first step. After that there is still a long way to real freedom. Real freedom means not only that your body is free; it means that your mind and your soul are free too.

The Negroes still had to win that kind of freedom.

They had to win the right to make a living. They had to win the right to an education. They had to win the right to vote and to hold office. They had to win the rights that free men had always taken for granted.

Even now, one hundred years after Lincoln gave them freedom, they do not have all these rights.

Even now as they toil slowly up the hard path of freedom there are some who try to delay them or to stop them—just as one hundred years ago there were some who tried to keep them slaves. Those people say, "Stop and rest, you have gone far enough." Or they say, "Don't try to go so fast; take it easy; there is time enough." Or they say, "You have gone as far as you can. The air is too thin up there on the high plateau of freedom. You can't breathe it. Stop!"

But people who believe in freedom know that if you stop to keep others from climbing the heights of freedom you keep yourself from climbing too. They know that those who withhold freedom from others withhold it from themselves as well. They know that freedom is like happiness; the more of it you give to others the more you have for yourself.

Twenty-five hundred years ago a great Athenian orator, Pericles, said that "the secret of happiness is freedom, and the secret of freedom is a brave heart."

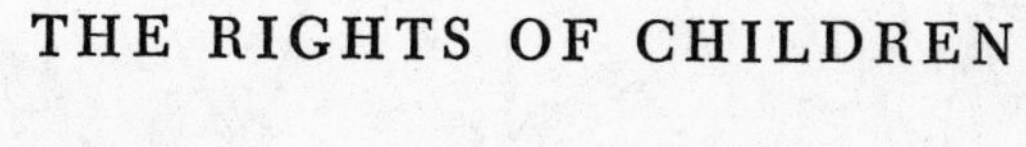

THE RIGHTS OF CHILDREN

If you were to make a list of the great discoveries of history, what would you put down? The discovery of America? Certainly. The discovery of the law of gravity—the law that whatever goes up must come down? Yes, that too. The discovery of electricity? Of course. The discovery of ether and novocain to take away pain? Probably. The discovery of outer space? Well, that's still going on.

One thing that you would never think to put down is the discovery of children.

How can you *discover* children? Children are always there. They have always been there.

That's just the point. Children are always there, so nobody thought much about them. But gravity was always there, too, and electricity, and outer space. And for that matter, America. But they all had to be discovered.

We know who discovered America, and who discovered the law of gravity and the uses of electricity and of ether.

But we can't say who discovered children. In a sense everybody did. About the time of the American Revolution and of Jefferson a new discovery of children was announced almost every day.

You have sometimes watched a pot of oatmeal or of corn meal coming to a boil on the stove. For a time all is quiet. Then there is a little eruption here—and there—each like a tiny volcano. Then the eruptions break out all over, and the whole pot boils and bubbles.

Philosophers decided to think about children for a change, instead of about grownups. Religious people started to worry about children's souls, and to set up special Sunday schools for them. Statesmen and reformers got anxious about children's health—they shouldn't be allowed to work long hours in factories. Teachers discovered that children had minds as well as bodies, and that their minds had to be fed too. Painters woke up to the fact that children were beautiful and that everybody wanted pictures of them. And storytellers turned to writing stories about children and for children.

Like Hans Christian Andersen.

Except that Hans Christian Andersen didn't have to *discover* children. There had never been a time when he hadn't known about them. What he did was to help other people discover them.

He grew up in the old town of Odense, in Denmark; not at all a bad place to grow up, with its soldiers in bright red uniforms at the castle, and a great church whose bells rang away at all hours of the day, and a little pond with white ducks on it. He lived in a house so tiny you could almost put it in your pocket, and his parents were so poor that they never knew whether there would be supper that night or not, but he was happy enough, little Hans. He had a patch of garden at the back of the house as big as a handkerchief, with a single mulberry tree, and he could sit out there in the summer and imagine that he was in an immense forest. He had a pair of scissors and paper and he cut out paper dolls and kings and queens and soldiers and animals and made a whole world for himself, and he made himself a stage and acted out the most elaborate plays—plays that he made up himself. His father worked away cheerfully enough at his shoemaker's bench, when he had any work, and when he hadn't he told little Hans stories or read to him from *The Arabian Nights,* and his mother, who couldn't read, took care of him and loved him dearly.

When he was only fourteen years old Hans Christian went off to the capital of Denmark, the lovely city of Copenhagen with its dozens of church spires covered over with green copper, and its gleaming blue canals, and with *real* kings and queens and princes. He was going to be a singer . . . he was going to be an actor . . . he was going to write plays. . . . My, all the things he was going to do and be. A fortuneteller had read his palm before he left home and said that someday he would be a great man and that when he came back home all Odense would be lit up in his honor. He believed that too: he could believe almost anything, and what is more he could make other people believe almost anything.

Such an ugly little boy—the original of the ugly duckling in his famous story—so awkward and gangling and bony, and so ignorant, too. People didn't know whether to laugh at him or to cry when he burst in on them and told them his many plans and hopes. In the end they all helped him, though—helped him to go to school, and to find work, and to travel and to make something of himself. They thought that in time he would stop being so queer and become a respectable young man.

But he never did, not really. He grew up to be one of the most famous men in the world, and the part of him that was famous was respectable enough. He dined with kings and with princes, he visited at country houses, he traveled in Germany and Italy and England and Spain, and wherever he went there were festivities and celebrations in his honor, even in Odense, just as the fortuneteller had said. But all the time the more real part of him went right on being queer—went right on living in a world of the imagination, a world that he created in his books and his stories.

What a world it was! A world where knives and forks talked to each other just as people do; where the moon stooped and peered into an attic window; where a lily sat down on a piano stool and played the piano; where fir trees longed to be Christmas trees, and then longed to be back in their cool dark woods again. It was a world where the brave tin soldier could fall in love with the beautiful paper doll; where shadows turn into men and marry princesses; where dogs had eyes as big as the Round Tower of Copenhagen, and where the tiny Thumbelina could fly off to Africa on the back of a swallow!

It is more real than the real world, this world of childhood that Hans Christian Andersen discovered—or made. It is the world of the Chinese nightingale who sang so beautifully that Death itself gave up and went away from the dying emperor; of the steadfast tin soldier who went rushing down the dark canal and was swallowed by a fish and then found once more by his owners; of the little mermaid who turned into a human being for love of her prince—you can see her sitting on a rock out in the harbor of Copenhagen even now. It is the world of the little match girl who warmed her hands on her matches and dreamed herself right into heaven; of the vain little girl with the red shoes; of the prince and the peasant boy who followed the lovely sound of a bell all through the world and finally met in a meadow high up in the hills; of the ugly duckling who turned into the beautiful swan. . . .

Hans Christian Andersen made everybody see that the world of childhood was just as real as the world of grownups. It wasn't that children were always happy in Hans Christian Andersen's world. Not at all. The poor little match girl froze to death, and the brave tin soldier ended up in the furnace, and the proud darning needle was broken into small pieces, and the poor mermaid lost her prince and was turned into foam. No, Hans Christian Andersen loved children too much to pretend that the world was always rosy and that, no matter what happened, everyone lived happily ever after. He loved them enough to tell them the truth. But it was *their* truth, about *their* world, and in *their* language.

That is what is so important.

Hans Christian Andersen's discovery of children was good for the children, good for everybody.

But that wasn't true of all discoveries.

Little Hans Christian had grown up in a country town. The father worked at his bench at home, and the neighbors all knew each other, and even when times were hard children weren't expected to suffer—or to work.

But with the growth of cities and the coming of factories everything changed. And as far as children were concerned everything changed for the worse. Oh, much worse!

For there was another discovery of children. Alas, it was a very different kind of discovery.

That was the discovery that children could work in shops and factories, in mills and in mines, just as well as grown men—and much, much more cheaply!

What a wonderful idea: to let children work instead of men. You wouldn't have to pay them but half as much as you paid their fathers. You could treat them any way you wanted to, because they were too little and too timid to answer back, or to stand up for themselves; sometimes the poor little things were almost too little to stand up at all. If they didn't do their work properly you could whip them or knock them about. They would never go out on strike against you; they would never make trouble for you. If one of them should fall asleep and catch his hand in the machinery, or lose the use of his legs from standing ankle deep in water all day, you could send him home for the town to take care of, and get another child to take his place: there were always more children.

It certainly was a wonderful discovery—this discovery that children could work in factories and mines instead of men. Of course it wasn't so wonderful for the children.

One day in the early 1800s a farmer named Richard Oastler visited some factories in the industrial city of Leeds, up in the north of England. What he saw horrified him. Little boys and girls of six and seven years old, standing up at the spindles twelve hours a day, six days a week, winter and summer alike. No time for school. No time for play. No time even for meals—the little things ate what was in their tin pails whenever they had a moment, while the wheels whirled and the machinery jangled in their ears. It was slavery, said Mr. Oastler—it was worse than slavery. Even slaves were better taken care of than that. Once he visited a factory with a planter from the West Indies who owned slaves himself. "I always thought myself disgraced by owning black slaves," the planter said, "but I never thought it was possible for any human being to be so cruel as to make a child of nine work twelve hours a day."

Soon Mr. Oastler got a banker friend, Thomas Sadler, interested in this child slavery. Together they went to the British Parliament. They stood up in the House of Commons and made speeches about conditions in the factories up north—about little boys and girls working all day in cotton mills and in pottery works. But nobody paid much attention to them, except to shake their heads at this interference with business. What! said the respectable members of Parliament. What! Interfere with the sacred right of factory owners to hire anybody they wanted? What! Interfere with the sacred right of parents to put their children out to work if they wanted? Why, that would be interfering with the way God had ordered things. Besides, if the children didn't work they would fall into bad ways. They would idle away their time on play or, worse yet, they would get into mischief. No, no, much better to let them work—better for everybody, better even for the children. In fact, they added, weren't the children lucky to have work at all? And they went off to their dinners of roast beef and Yorkshire pudding, with brandy and cigars.

But Richard Oastler and Tom Sadler kept everlastingly at it. Finally they got Parliament to pay some attention to what they said. That was in 1832. That year they got Parliament to appoint eight or ten of its members to see if things were really as bad as these tiresome men said they were.

Alas, they were worse. One by one the victims of child slavery came before the committee of Parliament and told their tales of woe. By now they were old men and women of twenty or twenty-five, broken and deformed by their long hours of work when they were children, and now thrown on the ash heap as useless. In the end the whole sickening story was spread before the people of England —and of the whole world.

It was a story of children working from ten to fifteen hours a day in pottery factories so ladies who must have tea wouldn't have to pay too much for their dainty teacups. Of boys working fourteen hours a day in hot, stifling cotton mills—no fresh air, no rest periods, no time to eat, beaten if anything went wrong—so mill owners could send cottons off to India at a handsome profit to themselves. Of children standing all day in water up to their knees combing out fleece so the rich could have their nice woolen blankets. Here was one boy of seven, from a mill in the city of Huddersfield; he got up in the dark and staggered to the mill a mile or so away. There he worked from five in the morning until seven or eight at night, with all of thirty minutes off for dinner, such as it was. When he got home he was too tired to eat supper, too tired even to talk to his mother. For that matter she was too tired to talk to him either, for she had worked just as hard and just as many hours.

Or here were children down in the mines—little tots of five or six, sitting down in the dark, opening and closing doors, or chasing away the rats. Older and stronger children—all of seven or eight years old, girls as well as boys, mind you—crawled on their hands and knees dragging little carts with coal through narrow black tunnels in the underground mines. Safety? That was their lookout. If something happened to one of them you could always go to the orphanages and get more poor boys or girls; the town was always glad to have them off their hands.

Or here were the chimney sweeps, hundreds and hundreds of them, and all of them little—no matter how old they were. England, in that day, was heated by coal fires in fireplaces, and that meant that the chimneys got clogged up with coal dust. The chimney sweeps—and only little children were small enough for the job, or children whose growth had been properly stunted—would wriggle up the chimneys and sweep down the thick coal dust. Of course the dust got in their eyes, and sometimes blinded them. It got into their lungs, and many of them died of lung diseases. And sometimes the chimneys were still hot and the little fellows got burned. Too bad. But chimneys *had* to be swept—how else could people stay warm and comfortable in their houses?

No, Negro slavery was not as bad as this!

Lord Anthony Ashley listened to all of these stories with horror.

He was one of the greatest lords in all England. His father owned half of the county of Dorset; his grandfather was the Duke of Marlborough. He was so rich he couldn't keep track of his lands or his money. He had gone to the famous Harrow School, and then on to Oxford; he was handsome and distinguished; he had married a beautiful wife, a great lady.

What a happy man, you might say. Not a care in the world.

Well, he was happy enough in his way, but he had plenty of cares; after all, being happy and being carefree are not quite the same thing. The reason he had so many cares is that he took on himself the cares of his whole society.

Young Lord Ashley had what is called *noblesse oblige.* There's no good English term for that, so you might as well learn the French. It means that those who are powerful and fortunate have an obligation to those who are weak and unfortunate—a special obligation that they must take on.

That's what Lord Ashley thought—that he was so rich and so powerful and so fortunate that he had a special obligation to the poor: to children working in factories; to pauper children in their miserable "ragged schools"; to women working long hours in mills; to miners working in dangerous places below the ground; to the insane who had none to care for them; and to many others.

Too bad more young men like Lord Ashley didn't have a sense of *noblesse oblige.*

When Lord Ashley heard about the children in the factories and mines he was terribly shocked. But he did not say, as you or I would say now, "It must all be stopped." He wanted to stop it all right, but he knew that that was impossible. You had to go at these things gradually, you had to win the public over to your side. So Lord Ashley introduced a law that no child under nine should be allowed to work, and that no one under eighteen should work more than ten hours a day.

You would have thought that everybody would have voted for Lord Ashley's law, but no such thing. There was a tremendous fight. The mill owners said they couldn't possibly make any money unless they could keep children on the job twelve hours a day. The miners said that they would have to close down their mines if they didn't have little children to pull the coal along the tunnels: men were too big for the job and you certainly couldn't expect the mine owners to enlarge the tunnels! And many men who sympathized with the children thought that it was dangerous to interfere with business at all. Things had to take their course. In time everything would come out all right—perhaps in a hundred years or so.

But now the working people of England were aroused. The little children of the industrial towns got together and serenaded members of Parliament when they came to see for themselves:

*We will have the Ten Hour Bill*
*That we will, that we will,*
*Else the land shall ne'er be still,*
*Never still, never still!*

Imagine marching and singing for the right to work only ten hours a day!

For Elizabeth Barrett Browning—she was Robert Browning's wife, and just as much of a poet as he was—the land was "never still" because there was always the sound of children crying:

*Do you hear the children weeping, O my brothers,*
*Ere the sorrow comes with years?*
*They are leaning their young heads against their mothers,*
*And they cannot stop their tears. . . .*
*They are weeping in the playtime of the others,*
*In the country of the free.*

It was hard to resist all that talk and all that singing, but Parliament wasn't going to give in all the way. So they thought up a brilliant compromise. "Let's draw the line at thirteen," they said, "not at eighteen. Thirteen is the real dividing line." As one dignified member of Parliament said: "Nature has drawn a sharp line at the age of thirteen. At that age childhood ceases, and the body becomes capable of enduring long labor." Think of that, all you children of thirteen or fourteen. So Parliament drew the line at thirteen —under that only eight hours a day, after that not more than twelve. There! That was a good day's work for the Parliament anyway.

Gradually things got better. Lord Ashley's bill was just the first of many bills to cut down the hours that children had to work. Finally there were laws that children had to go to school every day; that little children couldn't work in mills at all; that girls couldn't work in mines; that little boys weren't to be used as chimney sweeps. And somehow the spindles turned out their cotton, and the mines gave up their coal, and the fires burned in the fireplaces. So maybe it never had been necessary to use the labor of children, after all.

Children have rights—that was the lesson that the English learned, thanks to men like Richard Oastler and Lord Anthony Ashley. They have a right to play. They have a right to health. They have a right to be protected against abuse. They have a right to go to school. They have the right to be children.

Charles Loring Brace was another young man who had a sense of *noblesse oblige*. He too, like Lord Ashley, had been born with a silver spoon in his mouth. Not quite as big a spoon as Lord Ashley's, to be sure; after all, this was America, and there were no lords or dukes or castles or farms as big as all of Connecticut. But young Charles had money; along about 1840 he went to Yale College; he traveled abroad. He took a walking trip through England with Frederick Law Olmsted, who later built parks all over America so children would have some place to play. Charles wondered what to do with himself. One thing that he did with himself was to travel all the way to Hungary, where he somehow got mixed up in a revolution, and was put in jail, and had to be pried loose by the American minister and sent back home to his own country. As you can see, Mr. Brace was an impetuous young man.

Actually he took part in a revolution back in his own country too, but it wasn't called that. It was a revolution to save children.

Don't think it was just in England that little children worked in factories, standing by the looms or the spinning wheels ten or twelve hours a day. No, even in America, even in New England, where the good people were so worried about Negro slavery, they let children work harder than slave children worked in the cotton fields of the South. Even in great cities like Boston and New York and Philadelphia, where you would have thought there were enough men to do all the work, they used little children in the factories, because they were cheaper. Why, in 1832, when Richard Oastler and Lord Ashley were working so hard for the children of old England, two out of every five factory workers in New England were children under sixteen years old! Not until ten years later did Massachusetts get around to fixing the working day of children in factories at *ten* hours.

Later on a New England poet wrote a verse about them:

*The golf links lie so near the mill*
*That almost every day*
*The laboring children can look out*
*And see the men at play.*

No, even a rich country like the United States didn't take care of its children very well.

Look at New York. It was already the biggest city in the country, and growing bigger every day. It was like a growing boy whose clothes were never big enough for him, his arms sticking out from his sleeves, his legs too long for his pants. New York's clothes didn't fit, and there was no way even to patch them up. New York just couldn't build enough houses, just couldn't put up enough schools, just couldn't make room for enough playgrounds, no matter how hard it tried. And it didn't really try very hard. Every day, it seemed, new shiploads of immigrants would steam into Castle Garden in New York Harbor, and a thousand newcomers would stream down the gangplanks and into the city—Irish and Germans and Norwegians and Dutch, old men with bundles on their backs and women with babies in their arms and two or three tousle-headed youngsters tagging along behind, their eyes as big as half dollars as they looked about them at the New World.

Most of those youngsters were just like you. Their fathers found jobs, and their mothers kept house, and they went to school and grew up, just as you are growing up, to be about as nice as any children could be: anyway, that's what their parents thought. Most of them—but not all. For many of the newcomers couldn't make a go of it. The father died, or ran away, or took to drink . . . the mother fell ill . . . the family was broken and scattered. And the children? Well, the boys took to the streets and sometimes the girls too. There they were, the little street Arabs as they were called, thousands of them. Some of them sold newspapers, some of them carried shoeboxes and polished boots —that was really a necessity in the muddy streets of New York City. Some of them begged, some of them were little pickpockets. They ran around during the day, trying to earn a few pennies or to find something to eat; at night they slept in hallways or under the stairs, or broke into stores, or sometimes just curled up in a doorway like the little match girl in Hans Christian Andersen's story. They didn't belong anywhere. Nobody bothered with them or cared what happened to them—unless they got in trouble of course. They grew up as best they could, and if they didn't grow up—well, there were always others to take their place, so they were never missed.

Now we come back to Charles Loring Brace, that young man so eager to do good. He thought of being a preacher, and he even studied at a divinity school, but in the end he decided that preaching was too tame for him. Then he discovered the street Arabs of New York. He was only twenty-five himself at the time—not too much older than the boys themselves.

What was to be done for these homeless boys? First Mr. Brace got all his friends together and set up a society—the Children's Aid Society, the first of its kind in the country. He got clergymen interested in his work, and reformers and generous women who wanted to do something practical, and they all pitched in and helped. That was in 1853. The next year young Mr. Brace set up a lodging house for newsboys—and for other boys too; a place where they could get a bath and a bed and a supper and breakfast free. It went on for years and years, growing bigger all the time; in twenty years it had given lodging at one time or another to one hundred thousand boys: that's a lot of boys to need a place to sleep! But that was just the beginning. A night's lodging was all very well, but it didn't really go very far in taking care of homeless boys.

Next Mr. Brace set up special schools for the boys—evening schools where they could learn their letters and be warm at the same time; industrial schools where they could learn a trade. Then he had the happy idea of summer camps for these city waifs. You've heard of the Fresh Air Fund—your parents probably give money to it—which sends city children out to the country for two or three weeks a year. It was Charles Brace who started that, and of course it caught on and grew, like all good ideas.

Then came an even better idea. New York, and other big cities, had too many boys and girls with nothing to do but get into mischief. But out west there were never enough children. You can't really have too many children on the farm: there are always chores for them, and there is always food enough. Why not send these city boys to the farms? The idea caught on and spread. Eight or ten thousand of the street Arabs ended up as farm boys in Ohio or Michigan or Illinois.

"Be ashamed to die until you have won some victory for humanity," Horace Mann had said. Surely, as Charles Loring Brace looked back on his life, he was not ashamed to die.

Now turn to Chicago.

Chicago in 1890 was pretty much what New York City had been in 1850.

It was the fastest-growing city in America, and perhaps in the world. "Hog Butcher to the World," the poet Carl Sandburg called it, and it was that, and more too, with its flaming steel mills and its hundreds of railroad trains pulling in from all over the country, and the giant Great Lakes steamers filled with iron ore or with grain at the harbor. Everybody in the world knew about Chicago, and everybody in the world, it seemed, wanted to go there: Italians and Poles and Russians and Irish and Swedes and Bohemians. Why, there never was such a mixture: walking down Chicago's Halsted Street, you would think you were in the Tower of Babel.

And everybody so busy that there was no time for children, unless they could work too.

The little town of Cedarville was only a few miles from Chicago, but it was in another world of peace, quiet, beauty, comfort—at least for little Jane Addams. Her father was the first citizen of the town—even Abraham Lincoln knew him and respected him—and her home was the biggest and the finest house in town, and her garden had the tallest trees and the loveliest flowers. Yet even for little Jane life was not as perfect as you might suppose. She was pigeon-toed, and her spine was not quite straight, so she held her head on one side, and that made her very self-conscious. Nobody really noticed it, of course, but poor little Jane thought that everybody did. She didn't feel sorry for herself, though; she just felt sorry that her beloved father should have such a plain little girl. When they were out walking together she took care to stay behind a few steps so no one would notice her.

All that didn't matter, in the end. She grew up a pretty young lady, and went off to college, and then—because she had plenty of money—off to Europe to see if the rest of the world was like Cedarville, Illinois. You've heard what it's like to go abroad! Perhaps you'll go abroad yourself someday. Most travelers visit museums, cathedrals, palaces, the opera, famous restaurants, cafés on the boulevards, beauty spots in the Alps or on the Riviera . . . but not Jane! What she wanted to see in Europe was something very different indeed. She wanted to see "how the other half lived"—the slums, the ghettos in which the Jews were herded, the factories and working quarters, the hospitals and schools and orphanages. She knew that life wasn't all beauty and romance and she wasn't going to have it fed to her on a silver spoon. She herself wrote, with some sharpness, of "the sweet dessert in the morning, and the assumption that the sheltered girl has nothing to do with the bitter poverty which is all about her . . . which peers at her in the form of heavy-laden market women and underpaid street laborers." Imagine a little girl from Cedarville worrying about the heavy-laden market women and the underpaid laborers! How many girls who go over to Europe today do you think worry about things like that?

How hard life was for the poor; how drab and dreary; how filled with sadness and disappointment and heartbreak. What could she do to help? The same question, you see, that Lord Ashley asked, and Charles Brace . . . and the same *noblesse oblige.*

Then it was that Jane Addams had something like a vision. You can't do things *for* people—you have to do things *with* people. You can't be a Lady Bountiful, dispensing a bit of charity here and there and waiting for people to be grateful to you. You have to go and share their lives with them, as an equal—to suffer with them and rejoice with them.

Why not buy a house in the midst of the slums and settle down and live with the poor?

So back to Chicago she went. Not to the great Chicago along the shore of Lake Michigan with its palaces and mansions and boulevards and carriages and parks. No, to Halsted Street, near the stockyards—to Halsted Street where the Italians and the Poles and the Bohemians lived in tenements and back alleys and basement hovels—to Halsted Street, with its saloons on every corner, and its noises that never stopped, day or night, and its stenches that struck the nostrils like a blow. . . . In 1889 Jane Addams found just the house—a great old barn of a house which had seen better days and belonged to a lady named Mrs. Hull. Miss Addams bought it and kept the name: Hull House.

A name is what you make it. Nobody would ever have heard of the Hull family if it hadn't been for Jane Addams. But now Hull House is known everywhere in the world. Perhaps the only *house* that is known as well is the White House. It took lots of Presidents to make the White House famous, but Jane Addams made Hull House famous all by herself.

Jane Addams began very simply, by just being there, in Hull House: taking care of people . . . listening to them when they told their troubles . . . helping them out of their troubles . . . giving them a warm supper when they were hungry . . . finding money for them when they were penniless . . . going to court for them when they were in trouble with the law . . . finding work for a young man who had been fired from his job . . . picking up children who were playing hooky and sending them back to school . . . patching up quarrels between husbands and wives or between fathers and sons . . . sending a nurse around to an old woman who was ill . . . helping a young mother with her first baby.

What an endless round of work. That first year two thousand people came to Hull House every week, and most of them, it seemed, were in trouble. And all of them wanted to talk with Miss Addams.

Jane Addams quickly learned that it was not much use helping out in emergencies; there were always more emergencies. Not much use healing wounds or drying up tears; there were always more wounds and more tears. No, the thing to do was to put a stop to what caused the wounds and the tears.

But how? Well, first things first. The place to begin was Hull House. And whom to begin with? Why, children of course. Babies. Boys and girls. Young men and women.

First, then, a nursery for babies, so their mothers could have a little rest now and then, or go shopping or visiting. Then a kindergarten—how much we all owe to old Friedrich Froebel—to take the little children out of the dank cellars or away from the steaming washtubs. Then a boys' club to take the boys off the dangerous streets and give them a playground for games and a room where they could play checkers or dominoes, or monkey around with hammers and saws. An art class where youngsters could learn to draw and paint and model in clay and in stone: astonishing how many artists came out of these Hull House classes. A music class, and the pianos and the violins were going all hours of the day. Dancing classes . . . and even ballet: how graceful the little Italian girls were! And after a while a summer camp up on Lake Michigan where children from the slums could learn to swim and play baseball in the fields or cowboys and Indians in the woods.

All for the young. That might have been Jane Addams' motto—all for the young. She wrote many books—how she found time is one of the mysteries of her life—and one of them was called *The Spirit of Youth and the City Streets.* The spirit of youth is alive anywhere, even on Halsted Street; it will flame anywhere, even in the slums of the great cities. Let us cherish it, Miss Addams said, for it is the most precious thing in the world.

But all of this was still just binding up the wounds. How to stop the wounds from happening in the first place!

And besides, if there was this much to do just on Halsted Street, think of all there was to do in the vast city of Chicago. Think of all there was to do in the big state of Illinois. Think of all there was to do all over America. All the children who had no place to play; all the mothers who had no time for their children; all the fathers who had no work at all; all the immigrants without friends in a strange land—think of all the misery all over America.

So Jane Addams turned to the larger task of preventing evil instead of trying to cure it after it had happened. Boys and girls in trouble with the law, which neither understood them nor cared for them but treated them just as if they were real criminals. What to do for them? Why, stop treating them like criminals. Treat them like children instead. Set up special courts just to take care of them—courts which would act like a friend, not an enemy. And Miss Addams got Illinois to set up the first juvenile courts in the world—the first courts that were just for children.

Boys and girls working ten hours a day in shops and factories, instead of going to school. No wonder they weren't happy; no wonder they got into trouble. Miss Addams went down to Springfield and talked the lawmakers there into passing a law that would put an end to the labor of children in factories—the first one that really had any teeth in it and that meant business.

Women working night as well as day, long hours in factories, with the machinery whirring in their ears and the lights glaring into their eyes. Long hours in restaurants, running back and forth from tables to kitchen and back; long hours in office buildings, washing floors and cleaning up after all the businessmen were home in their comfortable beds. But women should be home with their families, not off working for a living at night. And Jane Addams pushed through a bill making it against the law for women to work at night. A judge in long black robes said, "You can't do that! Women can work any time of the day or night that they want"—just like those men in England who said that children should be allowed to work as long as they wanted. But in the end Miss Addams had her way—as she usually did—and mothers could stay home with their children.

The schools of Chicago were in a bad way—old buildings, poor teachers, no libraries, no playgrounds, even; the children could play in the streets or in alleys or not at all. In the Hull House district there were three thousand more children than there were seats in schoolrooms. What happened to the children? asked Miss Addams. She got herself elected to the school board and for years worked for better schools.

Garbage collectors didn't bother with poor districts like Halsted Street, and the garbage piled up on the street and the sidewalks until you could hardly walk around it. Miss Addams protested, and the politicians just laughed at her. So she got herself elected garbage inspector. Every morning she was up at six o'clock following the garbage wagon around the streets and alleys to make sure that the job was done properly. For the first time in history Halsted Street was cleaned up.

Wonderful Jane Addams, working away so simply and quietly there at Hull House. It was no longer just one house, for over the years it had grown and grown. By 1920 it was a whole village of houses—fifteen or twenty of them, each one as busy as a beehive. A hundred thousand boys and girls and men and women went through its doors every year—to draw, to paint, to dance, to play the piano, to learn how to take care of babies or to sew or to read. Professors from universities and social workers and judges came and lived at Hull House for months at a time in order to learn what Jane Addams learned—how to work *with* people and live *with* people; many of them went off and started other houses like Hull House in other cities. Now all the world knew about Hull House, and no clever visitor from Europe or Asia thought that he had seen America unless he had visited Hull House and talked with Jane Addams.

If she had time to talk with him.

She might be tending a baby, or reading to some children, or encouraging a little Italian boy to play the violin. . . . Or she might be writing a speech for a meeting in London, or telling some congressman how he should vote, or writing a letter to the President of the United States. And you can be sure that the President read it. He not only read it; he probably did what Miss Addams asked him to do.

For example Miss Addams wrote President Taft that children were the responsibility of the whole country and that there ought to be someone in Washington who would see to it that the rights of children were taken care of everywhere in the country. And President Taft set up a Children's Bureau, and the lady he invited to take charge of it was Julia Lathrop, who had worked for twenty years with Jane Addams in Hull House.

There were two other things that were close to the heart of Jane Addams. One was the rights of women; the other was peace. In her mind the two were really one, like two sides of a penny.

The great war of 1914–18 came as a terrible shock to Miss Addams. How could human beings turn into savages this way? How could they go about tearing down the civilization that they had built up over the centuries?

It wouldn't have happened, she thought, if women had been in charge.

Women thought first of their children. After all, children didn't make wars. Why should they be the ones to suffer? Men made wars, and they didn't stop to think of children. When they dropped bombs on cities they didn't stop to think that the bombs could kill little children along with grownups. When they put a ring of ships around a country so no food could get in, they didn't stop to think of the children who would starve to death.

But women would think of these things first.

All the last years of her life Jane Addams spent working to save the helpless victims of war—working for the League of Nations, working for peace. She thought that the best way to make sure of peace was to see to it that women were able to vote, everywhere. Women would vote against war—that she was sure of. Give the women the vote; organize them all into one great peace society. Then maybe wars would stop.

She lived to see women win the vote in the United States and in most other countries. She lived to see the women of America and Europe and India band together for peace.

She lived to win the Nobel prize for peace—the greatest of all prizes.

She died before World War II swept over the world, killing women and children by the millions.

Perhaps that was just as well.

Children everywhere. Sick children. Crippled children. Blind children. Starving children. Motherless children. Children without homes. Children wandering along the dusty roads with nowhere to go. Children alone and lost.

Babies wrapped in rags, lying on the ground, crying for food. Little children toddling around in the ruins searching for scraps of food or sitting by the wayside crying their eyes out. Older children hungry and desperate, striking out blindly for themselves, hoping to find food before they starved to death.

World War II swept over Europe—over country after country, wiping out cities, smashing up houses, destroying churches and schools, killing millions of fathers and mothers, leaving millions of children by themselves. The war swept over the densely packed countries of Asia—China and Japan and Burma and the Philippines and others, wrecking and smashing and burning and killing, leaving millions of children by themselves. There had never been such ruin in all history. Never, in all history, so many children lost. Little things who should have been playing in the sun but who were too weak to play . . . children who should have been at school—but there were no schools . . . boys and girls who might have worked in fields or helped with the chores at home—but there were no seeds to plant in the fields and no homes where they could do the chores.

All ruined by war. All swept away by war.

In Europe alone thirty million children without food or clothing. Thirty million children close to starvation. Thirty million children weak and sickly, easy prey to smallpox and measles and tuberculosis.

Who would save the children?

Who could resist the cry of the children?

Everybody wanted to help . . . but how?

UNICEF. Those letters mean United Nations International Children's Emergency Fund, but no matter, UNICEF is enough. It carries its own magic. In Italy children think it means a cow because it brings milk. In Greece it means wheat because it brings bread. In India and Burma it means a gentle nurse, because it brings medicines and health. You know it, of course, here in America, in England, in Denmark, in countries all over the world . . . it means those lovely bright Christmas cards printed by internationally famous artists. It means trick or treat, on Halloween, with all the treat going to the children.

Once the world had waked up to the plight of the children, everybody wanted to help. Governments voted money; people bought Christmas cards; contributions came pouring in—money and food and clothes and medicine and toys and games and books—all the things that were needed.

Soon ships loaded with food sailed out from American ports. They sped across the Atlantic to the battered city of Hamburg and unloaded food for German children who were starving, and for Polish and Austrian children. They sped through the Straits of Gibraltar to the ancient lands along the Mediterranean, Italy and Greece and Algiers and Tunisia and Turkey, unloading food and clothing and medicine for the children. Soon planes winged their way out from great airports of London and Paris and Copenhagen, flying to the stricken children. They carried medicines and vitamins and cod-liver oil—and shark oil, too, which was thirty times as good—and they carried teams of doctors and nurses to rescue the children who were weak and sick and dying.

Everywhere you looked, there in war-torn Europe, there was UNICEF and with it other workers from the new United Nations who knew how to get farming started up again, and how to get pure water, and how to build houses and schools—all working together in the greatest rescue operation in history. Thirty million children . . .

Back in the United States and Canada the factories worked day and night to make the powdered milk and powdered eggs, and in Denmark and Sweden the laboratories worked day and night to provide the vitamins and the pills and the medicines. And off went the doctors and the nurses with their pills and vaccinations and injections—off to Poland and Italy and Greece and the Arab lands—and they pulled the dying children back to life, and made the sick children well and the weak children strong. They went off like armies, these doctors and nurses, to fight the diseases that had crept up on the children just as the jungle creeps up on the land if it is not held back—to fight malaria, which is spread by mosquitoes, and scurvy, which comes from not having fresh fruit or vegetables, and typhoid, which comes from bad water, and all the other diseases that were about to get the upper hand.

It was like a great battle—the battle against hunger and disease—and UNICEF won. That first year many little children died, but then the tide turned and the children were saved. They got their powdered milk, and after a time the cows came back on the farm and they could get real milk. They got their powdered eggs, and after a time the chickens were scratching in the yards, and they could have real eggs. They got their vitamins and their cod-liver oil, they got their vaccinations and their pills, they got their strength back. Gradually life picked up again: families came together, towns were rebuilt, there was food enough to go around, and wood and coal for heat, and blankets for the cold nights. The schools were rebuilt and UNICEF sent over schoolbooks and food for school lunches.

That was in Europe. There were still millions of children in Asia and in Africa—children who had always been hungry and cold and neglected, even in time of peace, and who were worse off now than ever. UNICEF moved in on them too, with food and with blankets and with vitamins and medicines—UNICEF with other teams from the United Nations: men and women working away to wipe out disease, to irrigate land, to save cattle, to bring in electricity, to do all the things that would bring more food and better health to backward peoples.

New hope for the children of the world.

Think of that next time you buy a UNICEF Christmas card.

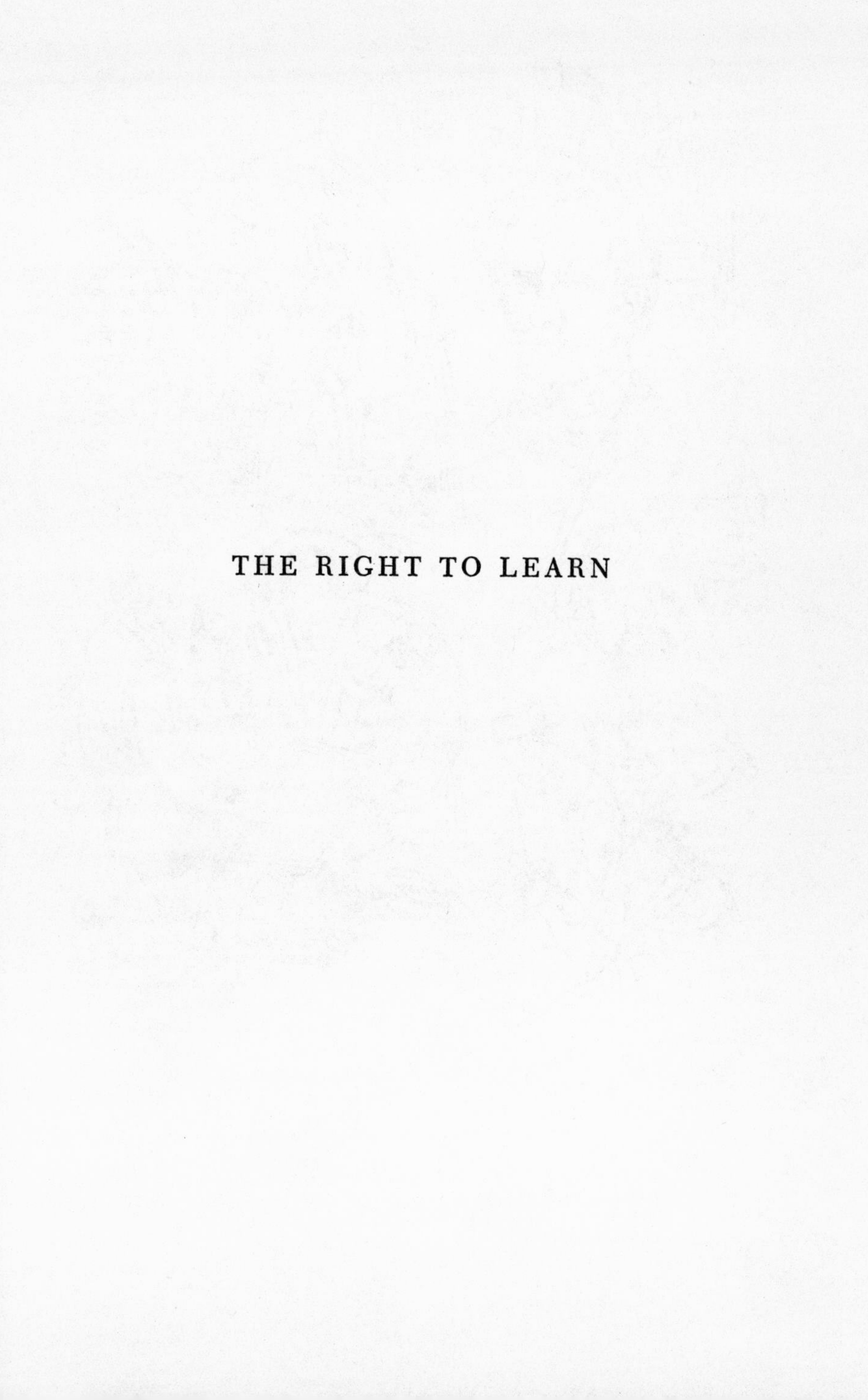

# THE RIGHT TO LEARN

HISTORY

One of the most important of all the discoveries about children was that they had a right to an education.

Of course in one way children had always had some kind of education. They had always been taught *something* —otherwise they wouldn't have lasted very long. Boys had learned to hunt and fish and swim and build fires and fight; girls had learned to cook and sew and take care of babies.

But when we say *education* we mean something more than this. We mean schools and teachers and books and study, and training and discipline.

Of course education, too, had been going on for a long time. But there are two things you can say about education during all the hundreds and hundreds of years from its beginnings in ancient Greece and Judea to just the other day. One is that very few people got any education at all. Poor people didn't need an education: what good would it do *them* to learn to read or write? Girls didn't need an education: learning would be wasted on girls. No, education was for the rich and the great, or for those who were going to be rabbis or priests and who had to know how to read.

And the second thing you can say about education is that mostly it wasn't much fun; neither for the children nor the teachers. Most teachers looked on children as little limbs of Satan; and most children looked on their teachers as their natural enemies. School was a kind of warfare between teachers and pupils. And no wonder. Drill, drill, drill; Latin and Greek; memorize and repeat, and a rap on the knuckles if you got it wrong.

So the world of children was pretty well divided between the great mass of children who didn't have a chance to learn anything and the handful of children who were made to learn things which they didn't enjoy and which weren't much use to them anyway.

Now if we are going to follow this discovery, that children have a right to learn, we will be racing all over the world: Germany and Chile and Denmark and Massachusetts and China—it makes you dizzy just to think of it.

Let us start in Germany, right in the center of Germany, in the ancient state of Thuringia, all hills and pine forests. And let us start with a young fellow named Friedrich Froebel. His father didn't think he was very bright, so it was his older brother who was sent to the university, while at the age of sixteen Friedrich went to work as a forester, in the thick Thuringian forests. Best thing that could have happened to him, too, for it meant that he learned to know nature. This was half of what he most needed to know in his lifetime.

The other half was children.

Some people seem born never to understand children. You'd think, to listen to them, that they had never been children themselves. All they can think of is: Oh, stop that noise! why don't you go out and play? stop asking so many questions! wash your hands! comb your hair! don't slouch! sit up straight! don't answer back! don't speak until you are spoken to! . . . And some people are born to understand children. Hans Christian Andersen, for example, who all his life thought and imagined things just the way children thought and imagined. Or Lewis Carroll in England, a fussy little old bachelor who lived with his Alice and his Red Queen and his Mad Hatter in his own Wonderland. Or Bronson Alcott over in America—but we shall meet him later.

Now here is Friedrich Froebel, a German born at the very end of the American Revolution, who fell in love with nature and with children. Almost by accident he got a chance to teach, and after that he was never the same. "I was as pleased as a fish in water," he said, and for him the water turned out to be the water of life. The first thing he did was to go off to the little Swiss village of Yverdon, where a teacher named Johann Pestalozzi was running a very curious kind of school. You wouldn't think it at all curious, because it is just what you are used to, but everybody in Switzerland thought it was curious, and almost everybody in Germany, too, except Friedrich Froebel.

What was curious about it was that Pestalozzi really liked children and that children really liked him. He liked teaching, and they liked learning.

And now here was young Friedrich Froebel to help old Pestalozzi and to work out some ideas of his own, too. Between the two of them, the Swiss and the German, they made a revolution in education. It was the most peaceful revolution you ever heard of, but it was a revolution all the same.

What Pestalozzi and Froebel said was really very simple: children are people too. Children have rights. Let them learn naturally, not by having things hammered into them. Let them talk if they want to—no silence in the classroom, or standing in the corner because they talked out of turn. Let them learn because they enjoy learning—no punishments because they don't know their lessons. Let them work things out for themselves, with their minds, and with their hands. Let them learn to use scissors and needle, hammer and saw. Take them out into the country and let them see how flowers and trees grow and how the birds build their nests and how the fish dart under the rocks in the streams.

Out of all this came a wonderful invention. It was Froebel's invention.

Froebel called it a kindergarten.

The kindergarten was just what its name says—a children's garden, a garden where each child would have his own little piece of ground to take care of. He could plant flowers and vegetables, water them, pull up the weeds, keep his garden tidy and beautiful. And he would learn lessons directly from nature. In the wintertime when he wasn't out in his garden he could learn to draw flowers and trees, or to cut out pictures of animals and birds, and then to spell their names and learn about their habits. Learning would be made into a game which teachers and children played together.

The kindergarten caught on, and soon everybody was talking about it. Soon visitors came flooding down to the little town of Blankenburg to see Herr Froebel's kindergarten. They saw that the children were healthy and happy, and that they were learning faster than at old-fashioned schools. Other teachers started teaching by the new kindergarten method, and soon the fame of the kindergarten went all over the world.

A new idea in education!

But aren't new ideas dangerous?

Yes, indeed they are.

So one day Friedrich Froebel read in the paper that the government had put a stop to all kindergartens.

Surely that was a mistake! Why should the government be afraid of little children playing in their gardens?

But it wasn't a mistake at all. The government really meant it. After all, they said, if you start with new ideas in school, who knows where you will end? Why, people might get in the habit of having new ideas, and nothing could be more dangerous than that. So let's stop all new ideas before they really get started.

Ah, but the government was too late. The kindergarten idea was already started!

Ideas are like wind. They blow around the world. There is no telling where they will go or who will breathe them into his lungs.

Over in America, Bronson Alcott felt the winds of new ideas about children and education blowing on his cheek and filling his lungs.

You know Bronson Alcott. You may not think that you know him, but you do, all right. He is the father of the Little Women—the father of Jo and Beth and Amy and Meg. And everybody in the world knows them.

Did you think they weren't real people, or that their father wasn't a real father? He was real all right, Bronson Alcott. He was one of the kindest and gentlest men you ever heard of; only a girl who had grown up in a happy household could have written *Little Women*.

But what an odd man he was, Mr. Alcott, absent-minded and simple-minded; he always seemed to be thinking of something else, far away. You couldn't trust him with any money because he would give it away to anybody who asked for it or needed it, and that was hard on his wife and children because they needed it too. You couldn't trust him to take care of himself either; once when a mob had gathered to rescue a runaway slave, and the soldiers stood at the courthouse door with their bayonets pointed, Mr. Alcott just walked up the steps and pushed the bayonets aside with his umbrella and said, "Why are we not within?" and went in.

He believed that everything should be simple—really simple—just plain living and high thinking, and when he said plain living you have no idea how plain plain could be. He set up a little community in a farmhouse that he called Fruitlands, not far from Boston, and everybody there lived plainly: whether they went in for high thinking is another matter. No meat, no sugar, no tea or coffee, no milk or butter, not even salt or pepper; all of those things were luxuries, thought Mr. Alcott. His daughter Louisa May remembered what they had to eat: "unleavened bread, porridge and water for breakfast; bread, vegetables and water for dinner; bread, fruit and water for supper." How would you like meals like that?

But Bronson Alcott was not such a simpleton as you might think. After all, everybody respected him, even men like Theodore Parker and Ralph Waldo Emerson. In some ways he was more sensible than almost anyone else. He didn't take things for granted, but worked them out for himself. He didn't take for granted that everything had already been thought of, but was quite sure that some new ideas were just as good as old ones, and maybe better. He wouldn't accept the notion that all men are naturally bad; on the contrary, he thought that all men were naturally good, and that if you trusted them and were fair to them they would not disappoint you.

And all that went for children too.

Just about the time Friedrich Froebel was opening his kindergarten over in Blankenburg, Bronson Alcott started the same kind of school in Boston. It was called the Temple School, because it was held in a room in the old Masonic Temple.

What a school this Temple School was: there had never been anything quite like it in America before. It didn't even look like a schoolroom—pictures up on the walls, and statues of gods and goddesses from Greek myths along the floor, and curtains at the windows, and chairs around in a circle instead of stiff desks lined up like an army. And it didn't sound like a schoolroom either. All the old ways of teaching were wrong, said Mr. Alcott; let's wipe the slate clean and start over again. Children were naturally good, not bad: just trust them to be good and they would. Then away with all punishments, away with the sharp voice and standing in corners, with the ruler and the whip! Well, not quite *all* punishments; if a child was naughty Mr. Alcott made him punish the teacher, and that, you may believe, made the child ashamed. . . . Learning was natural, as natural as walking or swimming, so don't make a chore of it, just let it come naturally. No drill, no memorizing, no drudgery; instead, conversations and songs and stories—not just from the teacher but from the children too. And just as in Froebel's school, the children were to learn with their hands as well as with their heads; there was to be picture drawing and modeling in clay and working with wood and with cloth, cutting and sewing and painting. And when the weather was good, walks in the park studying nature at first hand.

It was all too good to be true, and of course it couldn't last. It wasn't the government, as over in Thuringia, that closed down Mr. Alcott's Temple School, but it was much the same thing. It was people who said, "This will never do —imagine education being fun!" So they took their children out of Mr. Alcott's school and sent them to schools where they would really learn something, like how to spell "antidisestablishmentarianism," or to say "*Amo, amas, amat,*" and where they would be rapped over the knuckles if they got it wrong.

Of course in the end it was Friedrich Froebel and Bronson Alcott who had the last word. Now there are kindergartens everywhere, now every school is as pleasant as the Temple School. If it is not it ought to be.

Bronson Alcott wasn't the only man in Boston who was thinking about children and about education, any more than Friedrich Froebel was the only man in Thuringia who was trying to do something for children. There was one big difference between Boston and Thuringia, however, and that was that in Boston the government was on the side of the children. And of education.

Boston had such a long tradition of education that some people think Boston invented it. If Pittsburgh is the steel city and Detroit is the automobile city and Minneapolis is the flour city, Boston is certainly the education city. For three hundred years, now, Boston has manufactured and exported brains the way other cities manufacture and export automobiles or steel.

It all started when Boston itself started, back in the 1630s. Here is how one of the Fathers of the Massachusetts Bay Colony tells it:

> After God had carried us safe to New England, and we had builded our houses, provided necessaries for our livelihood, reared convenient places for God's worship, and settled the civil government, one of the things we longed for, and looked after, was to advance Learning, and perpetuate it to Posterity; dreading to leave an illiterate Ministry to the churches, when our present Ministers shall lie in the dust.

Almost the first thing the Puritans did when they came to Boston was to set up a school—it is still going, too, the Boston Latin School; maybe some of you are students there right now. And the very next year they set up a college and named it after John Harvard, who left it his library and a bit of money: that's one way to be immortal!

But the Puritan Fathers knew what nobody much in England or France seemed to understand: that you can't really build a roof before you have the foundations and the walls. And you can't have a learned ministry unless you start by teaching children their ABCs, and a bit more.

So in 1647 the Puritans passed a law that every town in the colony had to keep a school for its children, so that "learning may not be buried in the graves of our fathers." Well, that's not so much, you say, and perhaps not by your standards. But nobody else had thought of it. It was the first law of its kind anywhere in the world. *That's* much.

What a love of learning in the Bay Colony; yes, and in the other New England colonies too. Look over New England, and what you see is schools, academies, colleges. Why, when the Revolution broke out New England had more colleges than Old England. And New England was probably the only region in the world where almost everybody could read the Bible and the newspapers, and where almost everybody could speak up in public meeting, and make sense.

But somehow, after the Revolution, things got bogged down.

Education went backward instead of forward.

The towns began to feel poor, and stopped supporting their schools. They crowded their children into miserable, ramshackle buildings, cold in the winter, hot in the summer, with leaky roofs and drafty windows, and for playgrounds only a muddy yard. When they hired teachers they got the cheapest they could find—old women who had no other way to stay out of the poorhouse, or down-and-out men who knew nothing about teaching and cared less. Worst of all, the towns didn't even enforce the laws about going to school. Thousands of little boys and girls who should have been at school were working ten or twelve hours a day in factories instead.

What had happened to education in New England?

That's what Horace Mann asked himself. What has happened?

But he asked another question, too. What are you going to do about it?

Meet Horace Mann.

He is another of those people who believed in children.

But he was not in the least like Bronson Alcott.

He was as tough as an oak tree and as resolute as a ship driving through the waves. A tall, slender man with an immense forehead and burning eyes; when he made up his mind to something, he did it. At the age of nineteen he made up his mind to go to college—he had been a workingman since he was ten—and he learned enough in six months to get into the sophomore class at Brown University, and then in time he graduated at the head of his class. He made up his mind to marry the daughter of the president of his college, and he did, too. He made up his mind to study law and go into politics, and before he was through he was a senator down in Washington.

But all of these things counted for nothing when he made up his mind to save the schools of his state of Massachusetts. When he was through you wouldn't have recognized them as the same schools; for that matter you would hardly have recognized Massachusetts as the same state. And before he was through he had changed not only the schools of Massachusetts but of the whole United States, and of many other countries in the world as well.

He was that kind of man, the kind who knows what has to be done and then drives toward it. Nothing could stop him. Nothing could discourage him. Nothing could turn him aside. Nothing could frighten him. He was like a general commanding an army, firm and patient and brave, and determined to win at whatever cost. He was the George Washington of American education.

In 1837 Horace Mann got a new job.

The state of Massachusetts had finally decided that something ought to be done about its schools. But just *what* ought to be done nobody seemed to know. So they set up a Board of Education, and the governor asked Horace Mann to be in charge of it. The pay? Very poor. The duties? Well, everything anybody could think of.

Not much of a job for one of the leading lawyers of the state. Not much of a job for a state senator. But Mr. Mann didn't hesitate for a moment.

"Be ashamed to die," he once said, "until you have won some victory for humanity." Here was his chance to win a victory for humanity.

For humanity! Not just for the children.

Horace Mann was interested in children all right. But he was interested in them chiefly because they were going to grow up and be citizens and voters. How could they be good citizens or good voters if they didn't have a proper education?

Horace Mann saw what Thomas Jefferson had seen fifty years earlier—that the United States was trying a new experiment in the world and that education was part of it. It was an experiment in self-government. Everywhere else in the world people were ruled by emperors and kings, by generals and admirals, or by the rich and the wellborn. Education wasn't so important in these countries: just educate the kings and the generals and the rich, and the rest of mankind wouldn't need education. But in America it was the people who were the rulers. They were expected to run all their affairs. They were expected to elect governors and judges and presidents; they were even expected to *be* governors and judges and presidents! Everybody took for granted that the rulers in the Old World had an education, the kings and lords and bishops. Why not take for granted that the rulers in the New World should have an education, too—the farmers and workingmen and shopkeepers?

Education for citizens—that's what Horace Mann was thinking about day and night. Education so democracy would work. Education so the Republic would survive. After all, as he wrote, "the children of this people will soon possess the *rights* of men, whether they possess the *character* of men or not." That is, they would grow up to vote and to hold office, even if they didn't have any education. So better see to it that they *did* have an education.

With Horace Mann at the helm things really got going. Back and forth, across the state from Boston to the Berkshires, he went, stopping at all the cities and the country villages too, inspecting the schools, explaining to the people why it was to their advantage to have better schools. He persuaded the towns to vote more money for teachers; he saw to it that the schools were neat and clean and well heated and well run; he got high schools going in all parts of the state. He had been born in a town that took the name of Franklin because old Benjamin Franklin had given it a library, and when he was a boy he had read just about every book in that library. Now he set up libraries in the schools so other children could have the chance that had meant so much to him.

Then he had a brilliant idea. One reason so much of the teaching was so bad was that most of the town fathers who hired the teachers took for granted that *anybody* could teach: all you needed was someone who knew just a little more than the children. And as for knowing *how* to teach, why, there was no trick to it: just beat it into them. But Horace Mann had studied under some of these teachers, and he knew how silly that theory was. You had to learn how to teach just as you had to learn how to do everything else—cook or make furniture or practice law. So he set up schools to train teachers, the first in America. He called them normal schools, which was the French name for them, but pretty silly when you come to think of it, so we just call them teachers' colleges.

So much for Massachusetts, then. Things were looking up there. But Horace Mann was thinking of more than his own state, of more even than New England. He was thinking of the children of the whole country—children who would grow up to be voters and who would be running the country in another fifteen or twenty years. How to reach them?

Not everybody could hear Mr. Mann when he talked, but everybody could read what he wrote. So each year he sat down at his desk in Boston and wrote out a report on education. Each report was really a book—bigger than the book you are reading now. And it wasn't just a report on what he had done during the year; it was far more than that. It was a discussion of what *ought* to be done about education, everywhere.

Never had there been such a discussion of schools and of education as in Horace Mann's reports—twelve of them, before he was through. What should schools teach? How should they be run? How do you get teachers and train them for teaching? How can schools help make good citizens? How do American schools compare with French and German and English schools? These were the things Mr. Mann wrote about in his reports.

Everybody read them—everybody who counted, anyway. And almost everybody who read them sat down and wrote Mr. Mann a letter. Why, they had to put on extra postmen every time Mr. Mann sent out one of his reports! "Here is what our schools are like in Ohio," they wrote, or "Here is our problem in Virginia," or "How can we get the people of our town interested in their schools?" or "How do you get a library started?" And so many of them ended: "Won't you come out and tell us what to do?"

It was not only in America that men and women read Horace Mann's reports. They read them all over the world. They still do.

One day there was a knock on the door of Mr. Mann's house in East Newton, just outside Boston. When Mrs. Mann opened the door, there was a swarthy man with black hair and a black mustache. His name, he said, was Domingo Sarmiento, and he had come over from England just to talk with Mr. Mann. From England—with that accent? Well, really from Chile. From Chile? Well, really from the Argentine, but it was all very complicated. . . . Anyway he had read Mr. Mann's reports over in England and he couldn't go home until he had seen him.

That was the beginning of one of the important friendships in history.

For Domingo Sarmiento was no ordinary man. He was the Thomas Jefferson of his country—of the great country at the other end of the South American continent named Argentina.

Domingo Sarmiento was born in the Argentine, in the little country village of San Juan, nestling in the foothills of the snow-capped Andes. He was a village boy, just like a hundred thousand other village boys in a hundred thousand other little villages where nothing ever happened except the church bells ringing for early mass, or the winds blowing dust in from the pampas, or the wild cowboys riding into town and turning everything topsy-turvy. But something happened to him: maybe it was reading Benjamin Franklin's *Autobiography*—in Spanish of course—and wondering if he couldn't grow up to be like Mr. Franklin. "I felt I was Franklin—and why not? I was as poor as he, studied as hard as he, and managed to follow in his footsteps." So said young Domingo.

He didn't really follow in Franklin's footsteps as much as in Jefferson's. But then Jefferson didn't write an autobiography, so Domingo didn't know about him, not until much later on, anyway.

What an ardent young man he was. He started imitating

Franklin by getting himself involved in a revolution. That was easy, in the Argentine; there was almost always a dictator in power in Buenos Aires, and almost always a number of little local dictators lording it over some province or other—and almost always some kind of revolution. The difference between Franklin's revolution and Sarmiento's is that Franklin won and Sarmiento lost. Quite a difference. The wonder is they didn't put young Sarmiento up against a stone wall and shoot him. Instead they told him to get out of the country. Over the Andes, and into Chile: that's the place for you. Good riddance!

It was just about the best thing that ever happened to Domingo Sarmiento.

For it was in Chile that Señor Sarmiento really found his lifework—a work that turned out to be very much like Horace Mann's lifework. He started to teach; he wrote books on teaching; he set up a school for teachers. Pretty soon the government of Chile, which was much more sensible than the government in the Argentine, made him Minister of Education—much the same kind of job that Horace Mann took on. Señor Sarmiento knew that the Europe of his day was swirling with new educational ideas, so off he went to Europe to learn for himself: Switzerland, Germany, France—talking with people like Froebel and with that odd man who had invented the normal school, named Victor Cousin. Then, before he went home, Sarmiento crossed the Channel to England to see if he could learn anything there.

The most important thing that happened to him in England was that he read Horace Mann's reports on education. He was so excited that he went to Boston just to see Mr. Mann.

You don't usually get so excited about a book that you go clear across an ocean just to talk to the author. But then you aren't Domingo Sarmiento either.

In a way the United States went to Sarmiento's head, and he never got over it. He went back to Chile to carry through many of the reforms he had seen abroad, and he did, too. Then there was another turn of the wheel of fortune in the Argentine, and now they wanted the famous Sarmiento back home. So there he was, Minister of Education, with power to do almost all the things he wanted to do. But it wasn't easy. The Argentine was so far behind—everything had to be done from the ground up. In no time at all Sarmiento had built hundreds of new schools, and trained teachers, and set up libraries, and opened up colleges: it was a real revolution. And as for Sarmiento, he was so successful that they wouldn't leave him alone but took him away from his schools and sent him back to the United States as ambassador.

Horace Mann was dead now, but there were others carrying on his great work, and Ambassador Sarmiento spent most of his time learning about American schools. He saw how the new states in the American West started off with schools and colleges, and he saw how all the millions of immigrants pouring in from Europe were made into Americans by the American schools. That was what the Argentine needed—schools and colleges in the new states out on the pampas—and millions of immigrants who would be made into Argentinians. . . . And then there was still another spin of the wheel of fortune, and—well, remember what we said about Sarmiento being like Thomas Jefferson? Now he found himself President of the Argentine, just as Jefferson was President of the United States. He thought of all that Horace Mann had done, and he thought of all that Jefferson had done, and he knew that this was his chance to make the Argentine the United States of South America. He did many things, as President, but mostly he was an educator President. Mostly he did things for the children and the young people so that the Argentine could catch up with the countries of the Old World and with the United States.

Now over to Denmark, on the other side of the world from the Argentine.

Poor little Denmark! Somehow she had got mixed up in the war that raged over all Europe, and on the losing side! Here she is in 1815, at the end of her tether. Her territory is torn in two and what is left is almost too small to bother with. Her capital has been bombarded. Her treasury is empty. Her people are poor and, what is worse, they are in despair.

How save Denmark from going under?

That was what the young clergyman, Nicholas Svend Grundtvig, asked himself. And as nobody else had an answer, he found one. As nobody else seemed ready to save Denmark, he undertook to do it himself.

Or at least to call on the Danish people to do it *themselves.* When you call on people to do things they usually respond. But first there has to be someone with the vision to see what needs to be done.

Save Denmark by religion! And Pastor Grundtvig started a religious revival, speaking to his countrymen in warm, simple language that they could understand and calling them back to the churches. Save Denmark by remembering its glorious past—after all, it had a longer history than almost any other country. And historian Grundtvig wrote its history in words which everybody could read and which stirred every Dane with pride in his country's history. Save Denmark by telling the story of its myths and legends, the wonderful story of Norse mythology, of gods and goddesses like Odin and Thor and Freya. You know them well because they gave us the names of our days: Odin's day, or Wednesday; Thor's day, or Thursday; Freya's day, or Friday. . . . Save Denmark by songs and music, and poet Grundtvig—the greatest of all Danish poets—wrote lovely and thrilling songs that everybody could sing, and that sang themselves into the hearts of the people.

Above all save Denmark by education!

What do you mean, by education? Denmark already had schools, and all Danish children were supposed to go to them and learn their letters. What more do you need than that?

"A great deal more," said schoolmaster Grundtvig, "a great deal more indeed. Your schools are all very well for teaching the ABCs, and the multiplication tables, and such matters, but these are not enough. They are all right to begin with, but we must do more than begin, we must go on and on. Education isn't something that stops when you are ten or twelve years old; education is for life."

You see, Grundtvig was saying much the same thing that Friedrich Froebel was saying in Germany and Bronson Alcott in Boston and Domingo Sarmiento in Chile and the Argentine: old-fashioned education wasn't enough. But Grundtvig came up with a really new idea. There aren't many new ideas in history, so pay attention to this one.

Education didn't need to end when you had finished school. You could go back and start again, in a different kind of school.

He called it the Folk High School.

Not at all like the high schools you know, or like any schools that you know. Really more like the summer camps that some churches run nowadays.

The Folk High School was meant for youngsters of seventeen or eighteen. By that time they had been out of school for five or six years, or even more in some cases, and probably forgotten most of the things they had ever learned. And pretty soon they would marry and settle down for life on some farm or in some village, and that would be the end of them. Catch them, while they were still young and full of life and hope, said Grundtvig. Give them something to think about, these peasant boys and girls who might otherwise turn into drudges. Bring them together in the winter months, when work on the farm was slack, and let them study together and work together and sing and play together. Let them read the Bible for themselves, and discuss it among themselves. Tell them stories from Danish history and from Norse mythology and let them get interested in the past. Teach them how to read music and get them in the habit of singing: what a comfort that would be in the years ahead. And teach them practical things, too: teach the boys up-to-date methods of farming; teach the girls how to cook and bake and sew and keep house. Give them the habits of thinking and talking and reading and a sense of self-respect. Open their eyes to the world about them, open their minds to the world of learning, open their hearts to the world of their fellow men. Let them come to know the richness of life.

What an exciting idea—what an exciting program. But Bishop Grundtvig—yes, he was a bishop now—was far too busy to carry it out himself. He let his young friend Christen Kold do that.

Grundtvig was a remarkable man, perhaps the most remarkable man Denmark ever produced.

But Christen Kold was pretty remarkable too.

He was the son of a shoemaker, and his father wanted him to be a shoemaker too, but that didn't work at all. He was so clumsy that he couldn't even hammer a nail into a shoe without hitting his fingers, and he spoiled enough leather to make shoes for a whole army, anyway a Danish army. No, what Christen wanted was to be a teacher—never anything but that. He began to teach when he was only fifteen, and he did well enough, too. But he couldn't get a regular teaching job, because the men who sat in big offices back in the capital and ran all the schools said that he was too much of a dreamer. He might lead the young people astray! Just like Friedrich Froebel and his kindergartens.

It certainly is comforting, the way all the men who sit in big offices, with titles in front of their names and gold braid on their uniforms, worry about children being led astray!

True enough, Christen Kold did have a lot of odd ideas. Curiously, they were almost the same ideas that Froebel had in Germany and that Bronson Alcott had in Massachusetts and that other people had all over the world, so maybe they weren't so odd after all. Why should education be a matter of learning things "by heart"? Really the heart didn't have much to do with it; it was more like learning by machine. Why should children hate school? Why should the teacher and the pupils be at war with each other? Why not make school pleasant by playing games, and telling stories, and helping with the work, just as mothers did with their children at home?

Anyway you can see why those officials in the capital wouldn't give Christen Kold a job!

Then young Christen got a chance to go to Syria as a tutor—imagine, way out there almost at the other end of the world—and off he went. After a while he got tired of that, just as you would, and wanted to go home again. He had money enough to get on a boat to Italy, and there he bought himself a little go-cart and piled all his belongings into it and started to walk back home to Denmark. He did it too—over mountains and across rushing rivers and along valleys and through busy towns, hundreds and hundreds of miles across Austria and Germany, to Denmark. My, how glad he was to get home again.

When he got home he read about Grundtvig's idea for Folk High Schools. Just the thing, he thought, just what he had always wanted to do. So he hurried off to talk with the great man, and to get his blessing, which Grundtvig was quite ready to give. Then he borrowed some money and rented a house in the little town of Ryslinge, and in 1850, smack in the middle of the century, he opened the first Danish Folk High School. At first only one student turned up. Please, God, Kold prayed, let there be at least three so I can go on with it. And on opening day fifteen more came piling in, and his high school was launched, and with it one of the great experiments in the history of education. That's the way most things start: one man with an idea and with courage.

Soon Folk High Schools were popping up all over Denmark. Every young man and woman in the country, it seemed, wanted to go to the Folk High School. Almost overnight the Danish peasant was changed. He stopped being a peasant and became a citizen. He got interested in religion, in schools, and in politics. He became a better farmer—in time the best farmer in the world—and a better workingman, too, because he was a better man. Within a few years Denmark had come to life, Denmark had had a revolution.

How to save Denmark? Why, Denmark was saved. Denmark was prosperous. Denmark was democratic. Denmark had the best schools anywhere. Feel sorry for Denmark? Nonsense. Everybody envied Denmark. . . . And the Folk High School? It spread to Norway and Sweden and Finland and Germany, and to many other countries in Europe. It spread even to Asia.

Denmark lifted itself by its bootstraps.

But perhaps there wasn't so much to lift. A little country, a mere handful of people . . . why, forty or fifty Folk High Schools did the job for four or five thousand students each year.

Suppose you had four or five *million* students to think about?

Suppose you had four or five *hundred million* people to worry about? All of them a thousand years behind the times. All of them poor. Almost none of them able to read a page or to write his name.

How do you go about educating that many people?

If Yang Chu Yen had thought of *that* he might never have started his revolution. But he didn't—not at the beginning, anyway.

It all began rather by accident, this Yang Chu Yen Mass

Education Movement that was to make such a stir not only in China but all over the continent of Asia and in the island countries of the Pacific.

It began when young "Jimmy" Yen—the students at Yale College had called him Jimmy and the name stuck—went over to France with the YMCA right after the First World War, back in 1918. He had had the good luck to get over to America for an education, Jimmy Yen, and now he wanted to see if he couldn't do something for his fellow countrymen. There were a couple of hundred thousand of them over in France, brought all the way from China to take the place of soldiers who were fighting in the trenches. They were called "coolies," which means peasants and workingmen, and they were simple and poor and ignorant, doing what they were told to do, and feeling pretty lost, so far from home and from their wives and their children.

One day one of the coolies came to Jimmy Yen: please, would he write a letter for him, a letter to his wife? Needless to say, coolies couldn't write—only scholars like Jimmy Yen could write. And no wonder! Chinese is probably the hardest language in the world to write: you have to know thirty or forty thousand separate syllables or signs to write it properly. It's hard enough to learn the twenty-six letters of our alphabet, and how to put them together to make words, and how to spell all the words right; even now you sometimes make mistakes. Suppose you had to learn forty thousand different signs, or words, before you could read and write!

No wonder the coolies came to Jimmy Yen and asked him to write their letters for them.

Mr. Yen wrote the letters, all right, and then so many of his countrymen came to him that even if he had sat up all night every night writing letters he couldn't possibly have finished them all.

He had a better idea. Why not teach the coolies to write their own letters?

Was it *really* necessary to learn all forty thousand of the signs or syllables in order to read and write? Couldn't the Chinese alphabet—no, that's the wrong word—couldn't those Chinese signs be simplified, so that even coolies could learn to write their own letters?

What a sensible idea, and how odd that no one had thought of it before!

James Yen set himself to simplify the Chinese language, and after a while he got it down to only one thousand syllables. Even one thousand is bad enough, heaven knows, but if you work at it you can learn one thousand different signs for words: actually you recognize that many yourself without bothering to spell each one out each time; you don't really have to spell out e-a-c-h to get *each,* or t-i-m-e to read *time.* If you look at a word often enough or long enough you get used to it, just as you get used to a face, so you don't have to stop and make sure that the eyes and the nose and the mouth all go together.

So James Yen taught some of the coolies to read and to write, and as soon as one of them had learned he would go off and teach two or three of his friends. And then they would go off and teach *their* friends. It was like a chain letter, or a chain reaction. Soon there were hundreds of coolies over in France who were writing their own letters.

If you could do that with the Chinese in France, why couldn't you do it with the Chinese in China?

So in 1920 Yang Chu Yen—better give him his Chinese name back again now—went home to China with his big idea and his big heart, and started a revolution. He didn't mean to start a revolution, but that's just what he did all the same. For once the Chinese peasants were able to read and write, they would be able to do almost anything; once the Chinese peasants could read and write, things would never be the same in China again.

But what a lot for Mr. Yen to do before he could get started.

Have you ever thought of all the preparation that has gone on just to teach you to read? The hundreds of years of working out an alphabet. Inventing a printing press. Working out the right spellings for words, and the right grammar. Making dictionaries and spelling books and reading books. Training teachers and setting up schools and libraries. All just so you can read!

And in China? Nothing. No alphabet, no dictionaries, no readers, no schools, no teachers.

Nobody had ever thought of teaching Chinese peasant boys and girls to read. Reading was for scholars, as in Europe, hundreds of years ago, when—if you were lucky—you would learn to read and write in Latin. Reading wasn't for peasants. And reading certainly wasn't for girls.

Dr. Yen (for he was called that, now) had to select his thousand words; then write his own readers and spellers and get them printed; then build the schools and train the teachers. Even then he wasn't finished, for he had to go out and persuade the Chinese peasants that they ought to let their children go to school instead of working in the rice fields. What was still harder, he had to persuade them to go to school themselves.

But he did. Dr. Yen was quite a persuader. Before he was through he persuaded millions of peasants in many countries that they ought to go to school; he persuaded learned professors to go out and live in mud huts with their pupils; he persuaded the Chinese government to buy land for its peasants; he persuaded the United States Congress to give him twenty-seven million dollars for his work. They wanted to give him more, and he had to persuade them not to do that!

Dr. Yen started in the province of Hunan, almost in the middle of China, and he started by going right out to one of the villages and living in a mud hut just like the villagers.

For he had already learned what Pastor Grundtvig and Christen Kold had learned: that you have to start with the people themselves, by going out and living with them. That is what Dr. Yen did—and his wife, too, who was the daughter of a Chinese minister in New York. And pretty soon sixty men and women from the universities—students and even professors—came out to join in the great experiment.

And there was another thing that old Pastor Grundtvig could have told Dr. Yen if he had been there to tell it. It is this: that education can't be separated from the rest of life. It is no more a thing apart than your brain is apart from your body.

You can't educate children if they are at home sick. You can't get their parents excited about schools if they haven't enough to eat. You can't find teachers if war has come along and swept them all away. You can't build your schools if the men in your town won't turn in and help put up the school building and dig the well and do all the other work that is necessary before you have a real school. All of these things—schools and health and food and roads and water and the good will of the village or the town—are tied together in a single package.

But if all the difficulties are tied together, so are all the benefits.

Freedom from ignorance means better health and better farms and better homes, and even better government. And that is because, as soon as the peasants had learned to read and write and do a bit of figuring, they began to think and talk and discuss their affairs. If they could work together to build schools, they could work together to dig wells, or to clean up their villages, or to irrigate their lands. If they could read posters telling how mosquitoes carry malaria or rusty nails infect wounds or about the importance of vaccination against smallpox or the need to boil water before you drink it—if they could read all of these things, then they could cut down the diseases that swept away so many of their people every year, and kept so many of them weak and poor.

So Dr. Yen went all over China spreading his Mass Education Movement, until over eight hundred villages had joined it. It was like a snowball. Whenever Dr. Yen or his teachers had managed to train ten or twenty young men and women, they would, in turn, go out to nearby villages and teach ten or twenty more boys and girls to read and write. They would do more than this. They would teach them how to bring the soil back to life, and how to dig wells deep enough to get pure water, and how to protect themselves against illness and disease, and how to work together for the common good of the village. Dr. Yen and his teachers and helpers were doing what nobody had been able to do for four thousand years: they were breaking down the Great Wall of Ignorance that had cut the Chinese people off from the modern world.

Then came the World War. In 1937 Japan invaded China, and from then on there was nothing but turmoil and misery and poverty and war. The war went on for eight years, and after Japan was finally defeated, poor China was plunged into a civil war that went on for another seven or eight years, so for fifteen years China did not know peace. Dr. Yen kept right on, as best he could, training teachers and working away to wipe out diseases, and introducing modern methods of farming. He even started a college near the wartime capital of China, deep in the west. His work was so important that, when the United States voted hundreds of millions of dollars to help China, one tenth of it was set aside for Dr. Yen.

In the end the Communists drove out Dr. Yen and his teachers and workers. That was a pity, for he was changing the face of China; if they had let him alone he might have done many of the things they wanted done, without all the war and the death. But what he *had* done was not lost—what is done is never wholly lost. All those millions of peasants who had learned to read and write; all of those farms with new water flowing down from the hills; all of those babies saved from malaria and from the cholera: that was something. All those minds that were opened to the sun, all those lives that were saved: nothing could change that.

Dr. Yen had no idea of stopping just because he had to leave China. He moved on with many other Chinese to the island of Formosa and started up his Mass Education Movement there. Then on he went to the Philippine Islands with his great crusade. Here it wasn't so much a matter of schools and education—after all, the Americans had put in schools way back fifty years earlier when they took charge of the Philippine Islands. But after five years of war, and another ten years of poverty after the war, there was much to do even in the Philippines.

Dr. Yen used the same methods here that he had used in China. He went to the villages, little collections of huts tucked away in the outlying islands and almost forgotten by everybody except the people who had to live in them. In each of them he started what he called a "wiping-out" program: wipe out ignorance, wipe out disease, wipe out poverty. And he got the young people of each village to carry on the work. He had thousands of posters printed and put one of them up in each of the villages of the islands:

GO TO THE PEOPLE
LIVE AMONG THEM
LEARN FROM THEM
LOVE THEM
SERVE THEM
PLAN WITH THEM
START WITH WHAT THEY KNOW
BUILD ON WHAT THEY HAVE

Not so different from what Bishop Grundtvig and Christen Kold had said back in Denmark, a hundred years earlier.

There's one thing you can be sure of about children—and about schools—and about education—and that is that the job is never done.

You are one of the lucky ones. You know how to read—or you wouldn't be reading this book. And you live in a society that is rich enough to have schools and libraries and books. You live in a society that is rich enough to let you go to school, instead of sending you out into the fields to work.

Even after all the work of men like Friedrich Froebel and Horace Mann and Domingo Sarmiento and Christen Kold and Dr. Yen—even after all that, it is still true that most people don't know how to read.

*You* do, of course.

But China is at least three times as big as your country (that's pretty safe because China is three times as big as every country except India), and most people in China still don't know how to read.

Or in India. Or in Indonesia. Or in the Congo. Or in Brazil . . . and many other countries. Just think: most people in the world still can't read!

And just think: in many countries of the world they still haven't discovered children!

Curious how everybody seems to get the same idea at the same time!

For hundreds and hundreds of years nobody seemed to worry because the peoples of Asia and Africa and South America couldn't read or write. Education—so one might have supposed—was for white people only.

Then, just the other day, everybody woke up to the fact that all those millions and millions of men and women with black skins and brown skins and yellow skins were people too. Why not worry about them for a change? If it was a good idea for white boys and girls to go to school, why wasn't it a good idea for black and brown and yellow boys and girls to go to school? If it was useful for the men and women of Europe and America to know how to read and write, why wouldn't it be useful for the men and women of Asia and Africa to read and write?

For a long time people in Germany or England or America had said: "Education is for everybody." But they hadn't really meant it. They had only meant that education was for everybody in their countries.

Now people were saying, "Education is for everybody." And they meant *everybody*.

There was Dr. Yen over in France discovering that simple Chinese coolies could learn to read and write, and hurrying home to China to spread the good tidings.

And there was Dr. Frank Laubach, preaching the gospel in the jungles of the Philippines. Now he had made the same discovery, and he was getting ready to spread the news all over the world.

Frank Laubach hadn't planned to be a teacher. He had planned to be a preacher. The teaching came by accident. . . . Well, not wholly by accident, of course; things hardly ever do.

He had always wanted to be a preacher. But not an ordinary preacher: that was too easy, and he liked things to be hard. He wanted to be a missionary. But, again, not an ordinary missionary. He wanted to be a missionary in the hardest place in the world. He read that the hardest people to convert to Christianity were the wild Moros on the jungle island of Mindanao, in the Philippines. So of course he got himself sent out there. And he quickly found out that, sure enough, they *were* the hardest people to convert. So hard that he stayed there for years and didn't convert a single one of them.

He didn't even make any friends. That saddened him. Then one day he had a kind of vision.

Why should the Moros like him or accept the religion he

preached? After all, he didn't really like them, and he certainly didn't accept *their* religion.

In fact he didn't even know their language.

Imagine an Arab coming to your home town and trying to convert you to the Mohammedan religion—by talking to you in Arabic! He wouldn't get very far, would he? He wouldn't get a bit further than Frank Laubach got with the Moros there in the jungles of Mindanao.

So the Reverend Frank Laubach decided on two things.

First, that he must learn to like the Moros—*really* like them. That meant he would have to live with them, and live the way they lived, and be interested in the things they were interested in.

And that meant, of course, the second thing: that he would have to learn the Moro language so he could understand them and talk with them.

But how? Nobody had ever bothered to write down the Moro language. In fact, there wasn't even a Moro alphabet.

How do you set about learning a language if there isn't any alphabet and if there aren't any written words?

That really put Dr. Laubach to the test. It was just the kind of *hard* problem that he liked.

He solved it of course, and with the greatest of ease.

He wrote the alphabet himself. Then he wrote out the words of the Moro language.

Imagine inventing an alphabet! Imagine inventing a written language—for that was what Frank Laubach was doing!

Now everybody was delighted, most of all the Moros themselves. These fierce warriors who had terrified all the other Filipinos on the island were like children with a new toy. Now they all wanted to learn their language . . . learn to read it and write it. So next Dr. Laubach had to invent a way to teach it. He managed that too—he always managed everything he put his mind to. He did it by drawing pictures of the sounds and writing out the words next to the pictures. But that was only the half of it. The other half was to encourage the Moros to learn, and he did *that* by what you might call the "glad-hand" method. A warm handshake, a pat on the back, a gleaming smile, and at every sign of progress more handshakes, more pats on the back, more smiles and laughter. . . . It all worked like a charm.

But of course Dr. Laubach couldn't teach all the Moros to learn their language—that would have taken a lifetime. So like James Yen over in France he hit on the idea of making each of his pupils into a teacher.

He called his method "Each One Teach One."

Each one who learned the Moro language would go out and teach it to one other Moro . . . and he would teach it to still another . . . and so on, until everybody had learned. It was all that simple.

When some of the Moro tribesmen hung back because they didn't want to be teachers, one of the chiefs came to Dr. Laubach's help. He was a very important chief, too, so important that he had thirteen wives. "Everyone has got to teach," he said. "If he doesn't teach, I'll kill him."

That helped.

In no time at all most of the Moro men were able to read and write.

Then off Frank Laubach went, to other parts of the Philippines, to remote corners where no missionaries had ever been. Everywhere he went he discovered new languages—dozens of them—and he drew up alphabets and made lists of words and drew pictures that looked like the words. And everywhere he used his Each One Teach One system. And lo and behold, pretty soon almost everyone was reading and writing.

By now the fame of Dr. Laubach had spread all over the world. Every mail brought him a new invitation to come to some new country and teach the native peoples to read. So off he went—to Malaya, to India, to Ceylon, to Java. . . . That was twenty years ago, and Frank Laubach has been going ever since. Up and down the great country of India with its dozens and dozens of different languages, and to the neighboring countries of Pakistan and Ceylon as well. Deep into the heart of Africa: once when he was exactly on the Equator he jumped back and forth a thousand times, just so he could say, "The Equator was at my mercy." During the World War he went over to the West Indies, and into South America, to ancient Yucatan, to Peru, to Brazil. And then after the war back to Asia and Africa, to the countries on the Mediterranean, on the Indian Ocean, on the Pacific, a white-haired old man with a battered suitcase and a portable typewriter, conquering the world. Remember Thomas Paine said, "Where Liberty is not, there is my country"? Frank Laubach might have said, "Where Learning is not, there is my country."

Everywhere he went he used the same methods that he had used with the Moros back on the island of Mindanao. He had an artist with him now, and the artist would draw the pictures of words and sounds, and then write them out, and in no time at all people who thought they couldn't read a word were reading schoolbooks. Sometimes Dr. Laubach had to write the books too—just as Dr. Yen had had to write the books for his Chinese readers. But that didn't worry him at all: he liked to write books. And everywhere he went he used his chain-letter method of Each One Teach One.

Before he was through he had taught almost sixty million people to read.

Remember the story of Mr. Chips? He had started teaching in a little English school as a very young man, and he went on and on for fifty years, teaching the sons and the grandsons of his first pupils. And when as a very old man he lay dying, he heard someone say, "What a pity he never had a son," and he raised his old head, and his eyes flashed, and he said, "I had thousands of them, thousands of them."

Think what Jimmy Yen and Frank Laubach could have said:

"Millions of them, millions of them."

# THE RIGHTS OF WOMEN

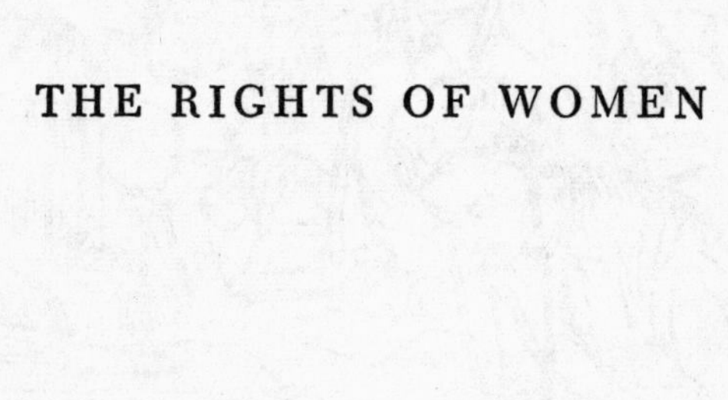

ELECTION THIS DAY
WOMEN WAN'T VOTE
WE DEMAND EQUAL RIGHTS
EQUAL RIGH FOR WOMEN

You know all about the Declaration of Independence of 1776. You may even know it by heart: "When in the course of human events . . ."

But did you ever hear of the Seneca Falls Declaration of Independence of 1848?

It was not *quite* as important as the Declaration that Thomas Jefferson wrote but it was important enough. It was the Women's Declaration of Independence.

Women's Declaration of Independence! What were *they* declaring independence of, anyway?

Men!

No, not quite the way you think. The women who drew up and signed the Declaration of Independence weren't a lot of disgruntled old maids; not at all. In fact the lady who wrote it was happily married and the mother of seven children.

No, what they wanted was very simple. Not independence from men, but independence from the *tyranny* of men.

"We hold these truths to be self-evident . . . that all men and women are created equal." That's what they said, and that's what they meant.

What do you think of that?

What you think of it is no doubt that it is all pretty silly. *Of course* men and women are created equal. Who ever thought that they weren't?

Of course girls can go to school, just like boys!

Of course women can speak up in public, just like men!

Of course women can be nurses or doctors or lawyers if they want to!

Of course women can earn money and keep what they earn!

Of course women can vote!

But there was no "of course" about it . . . not in 1848 when the women got together and issued their Declaration of Independence.

Odd as it may seem, the notion that women are the equals of men is something quite new in history. The notion that women should vote and hold office is so new that your grandfather and grandmother can remember when it all came to pass.

It is all so new that in many countries of the world it hasn't happened even yet.

No, for hundreds of years men had it all worked out—and very neatly, too.

Woman's place was in the home. Women didn't have any business meddling in the affairs of men—and almost all affairs were the affairs of men. Women didn't need to earn money, or to have property of their own, or to be doctors or lawyers, or to vote. Their fathers, their brothers, their husbands would take care of them. Just trust the men to take care of everything.

But it was the men who hired little children to work in

the mines and the mills. It was the men who stole Negroes from Africa and sent them over to America to be slaves, and who kept them working in the fields. It was the men who put up the slums in the great cities for women and children to live in. It was the men who set up schools and then kept girls out of them. It was the men who burned people at the stake if they didn't worship the right way. It was the men who waged wars . . . who wiped out helpless people like the Indians . . . who burned down towns and villages. And of course it was the men who made the laws saying that men were superior and women were inferior, and that that was nature's way!

Were men really to be trusted with everything?

Wouldn't women do better than that?

Anyhow they could hardly do worse!

Certainly that's what Elizabeth Cady Stanton thought. Naturally. She was the one who had written the Women's Declaration of Independence in the first place.

She was the daughter of the leading lawyer in the town of Johnstown, New York, and when she was just a little girl she had seen her friend Flora Campbell—Flora did the washing and the housework for the Cadys—walk away from her father's law office with tears streaming down her cheeks. Little Eliza ran after her to find out what was the trouble. Flora owned a house, and now her no-good husband was going to sell it, and they would have no place to live. And Judge Cady had said that there was nothing in the world he could do about it. Married women didn't own anything. Everything they owned belonged to their husbands. That was the law. And the law said that the husbands could do anything they pleased with their wives' property!

"Never mind," said Eliza, "I'll go and find the law and cut it out of the book, and then you can keep your house."

She did, too—but that was many, many years later.

Little Eliza grew up to be young Miss Cady, as clever a

young lady as you could find between New York and Buffalo. When she had learned everything the schools in Johnstown could teach her, her father bundled her off to the new seminary in Troy that Emma Willard had just opened up, and in no time at all she had learned all that the Troy seminary could teach her too. . . . Then what? . . . Then nothing at all, for there was no college in the country that would accept girls, no matter now clever they were. So there was nothing for Miss Cady to do but put away her books and go home and keep house for her father and play the piano and pour tea and walk in the garden and wait for someone to come along and marry her.

She didn't have to wait very long, pretty and clever as she was, and in 1840 she married a handsome young lawyer named Henry Stanton, being careful to leave out the "obey" from "love, honor, and obey" in the marriage lines. . . . Then off they went on their honeymoon, to London. Henry Stanton was a delegate to the world anti-slavery convention there, and he thought his bride could enjoy the sights of London while he sat and listened to what William Lloyd Garrison and Wendell Phillips and the English abolitionists had to say.

It didn't work out that way at all.

Elizabeth had no notion of seeing the sights of London while her husband was at the anti-slavery convention. That would be missing all the excitement. She went to the meetings of the convention herself, and it changed her life.

She had expected to hear the great orators of England and America declaim on the wickedness of slavery and say what was to be done to put an end to it. Instead she heard them spend their time discussing the wickedness of *women*, and deciding how to keep them from having any part in the crusade against slavery. Those troublesome Americans had sent over a number of *women* as delegates and the silly women expected to sit up on the platform, to speak their minds, even to vote . . . just as if they were men! That would never do—why, that would make the whole anti-slavery movement ridiculous.

To be sure, a woman sat on the throne of England: Queen Victoria herself. A woman could sit on a throne but not on a seat in their convention! So the convention solemnly voted that the women would have to sit off by themselves in the gallery, or behind a curtain, so nobody would see them, and they couldn't talk at all.

They wouldn't have treated slaves that way.

Unless, of course, they had been women slaves.

That was the first thing that happened to Mrs. Stanton there in London. The second thing was just as important. She met Lucretia Mott.

Now we must stop and get acquainted with Lucretia Mott even if it does interrupt the story of Mrs. Stanton.

Lucretia was a Nantucket girl. Nantucket girls learned early to be self-reliant and stouthearted. They had to: their menfolk were away on whaling voyages for two or three years at a time and everything was in their hands. And Lucretia was a Quaker girl, and Quaker girls, too, learn to be self-reliant and independent, to listen to the "inner voice," to go the way their conscience tells them to go, no matter what the world says. When Lucretia was thirteen she went to study at a girls' seminary, and stayed on to teach. She met James Mott there, and married him at eighteen, so she ought to have been pleased. Perhaps she was. But what impressed her most was that she taught just the same things the men taught, but got only half the pay that the men received.

Lucretia never quite got over that lesson.

She gave her life to teaching, and to crusading against slavery, but she gave her life to the crusade for women's rights, too.

She was there in London when they decided to put the women off the platform and away from the main hall, behind a curtain. Of course as soon as Mrs. Mott sat on one side of a curtain, it was all the people who sat on the other side who were behind it. They didn't realize that then, but we do now.

Mrs. Mott didn't get a chance to talk from the platform at the London convention, but that wasn't so important. What was important was that she got a chance to talk to the delegates—and their wives.

Especially Henry Stanton's young wife, Elizabeth Cady. It was clear that Mrs. Mott liked her and trusted her. And as for Elizabeth, it was the most important thing that ever happened to her.

There was a kind of apostolic laying on of hands. There was a passing on of the torch—from Lucretia Mott to Elizabeth Cady Stanton.

Now it is eight years later, and we can go back to Mrs. Stanton and her Declaration of Independence. She had moved from Boston with its ceaseless excitement over slavery and the lot of the Negro to the little town of Seneca Falls just a few miles from lovely Lake Seneca in upstate New York. Even here all her friends were excited about ending the slavery of the Negro. Was no one interested in ending the slavery of women?

Slavery! Wasn't that too strong a word?

Well, Elizabeth Stanton and Mrs. Mott didn't think so, and they ought to know because they had been thinking about it since they were girls.

In 1848 they put their heads together and decided that the time had come to do something about the position of women in America. And that meant a convention. In those days, when you wanted something done you always called a convention, and if you were anybody at all you spent all your spare time going to conventions—and even time that you couldn't spare.

This was to be a women's rights convention.

Soon men and women were streaming into the little town

on the edge of Lake Seneca—one famous name after another. None more famous than Lucretia Mott, though, unless it was the fiery Negro orator, Frederick Douglass, so tall and handsome and with a voice like an organ.

What to do? What better to do than issue a Women's Declaration of Independence?

Elizabeth Stanton sat down and wrote it; she followed Jefferson's Declaration as closely as possible:

"We hold these truths to be self-evident: that all men and women are created equal." There, that was a good start. Then:

"The history of mankind is a history of repeated injuries on the part of man toward woman." What injuries?

He had never allowed her to vote.

He had made laws in which she had no voice.

He had made her pay taxes without representation.

He had taken from her all her rights in property, even the wages she earned.

He had kept all the professions for himself and refused to let women be preachers or doctors or lawyers.

He had denied her an education.

He had put her in an inferior position . . . and kept her there.

All true enough, too, that was the sad part of it. Mrs. Stanton and Mrs. Mott weren't just two crackpots; the facts were on their side.

But it was one thing to declare independence and draw up a long list of wrongs and injuries. It was quite another to know what to do to make things better.

"We insist," said the women at the convention, "on all the rights that belong to citizens of the United States!"

Did that mean the right to vote? Certainly it did, said Elizabeth Stanton. And she put it to the convention: women have "the sacred right to vote." There was quite a stir over that one. What boldness! What audacity! Wasn't that going too far? Then up stood Frederick Douglass with his magnificent voice. Slavery was just as bad for women as it was for Negroes, he said. One way to end it was by giving everybody the vote—including women. With Mr. Douglass' help, Elizabeth Stanton carried the day.

So the great crusade was on: Women's Rights! Votes for Women!

It didn't get very far—not then. But what Abraham Lincoln later said of the Declaration of Independence itself we can say of this Women's Declaration of Independence. "They meant to raise a standard maxim for a free society; something everyone could know and test by."

Daniel Anthony was a successful businessman.

But he was a Quaker and a reformer, too, active in all good causes. One day Daniel Anthony came down from nearby Rochester to see Mrs. Stanton, and he brought his daughter Susan with him.

It was a case of love at first sight. Or, if not love, something as strong as love, and as enduring. For from that day on—it was in 1851—the two women were inseparable.

Jefferson and Madison; Sam Adams and John Adams; Lee and Jackson . . . even these didn't work together more closely than Susan Anthony and Elizabeth Stanton. And their alliance lasted for fifty years.

What a pair they were: so much alike in their faith and their hopes, so unlike in their character and their methods. Elizabeth with her husband and her seven children and her grandchildren; with her endless interest in lecturing and writing and editing; with her vivacity and excitement and charm. And Susan, an old maid, married to the cause of women's rights, and content to give her life to that cause, quiet, modest, hard-working, and single-minded—in fact with all the Quaker virtues. Each one was a tower of strength; together they were like an army.

"Never forget," Mrs. Stanton said later, "that if I have done anything for the women of my country, it is not I; it is Susan and I." And how beautifully they worked together, Susan all facts and figures and patience and planning, and Elizabeth all enthusiasm and energy and eloquence. There would be an important convention and Susan would persuade Elizabeth that she simply had to make the keynote speech—and then Susan would get up all the necessary material for the speech. There would be a meeting of a committee at the legislature, in Albany, perhaps on the right of women to own property, and of course Elizabeth would be the one to go down and argue the case, but it would be Susan who found all the facts and figures for her. . . .

But don't think that Susan Anthony was just a glorified secretary. Not at all. She was a person in her own right, was Susan, and as the years went on and Elizabeth got involved in editing that odd magazine called the *Revolution*, or in lecturing, more and more of the work fell on the tireless Susan, and more of the responsibility too.

Thus it was Susan who decided that the time had come to go on and vote, no matter what happened. And one fine day in 1872 she showed up at the voting booth, with no less than sixteen other ladies of Rochester, and announced that they were all going to vote and nobody could stop them. Nobody did, either—not just then. To be sure a few weeks later she was arrested for illegal voting—which is just what she wanted to happen—and in due course of time she was tried and found guilty and fined one hundred dollars. "I won't pay," she said, "nobody will ever make me pay." And she didn't either. The judge, who had hoped to make an example of her, didn't have the courage to send her to jail.

And it was Susan, too, who went out west to persuade the new states to give votes to women. Wyoming had led the way, in 1869, even before it was a full-fledged state. Soon Utah followed, and then Colorado, and one by one the other territories and states out in the Far West.

Neither Elizabeth Stanton nor Susan Anthony lived long enough to see women's rights at full tide, but both of them lived long enough to see the turn of the tide.

Once when Susan Anthony was still teaching school she went to a meeting of Rochester teachers where the men (remember women were supposed to be seen but not heard) discussed the question of why teachers were not respected as much as lawyers or doctors. Susan stood it as long as she could; then she got up to say just one sentence: "As long as society says that woman has not brains enough to be a doctor or a lawyer or a minister, but has plenty of brains to be a teacher, then every man who is a teacher admits that he has no more brains than a woman."

*Brains* enough to be a teacher? *Brains* enough to be a doctor or a lawyer? It wasn't as simple as that. It took more than brains to be a teacher or a doctor or a lawyer. It took education and training. How was any woman to teach anything beyond the ABCs, or be a doctor or a lawyer or a preacher, if she wasn't allowed to have an education?

Education! Education for girls! Education for women!

Girls were allowed to go to school, of course—up to a point. They were expected to learn reading and writing and a bit of arithmetic—enough reading to read the Bible; enough writing to write letters; enough arithmetic to add up the grocery bill. But after that?

Well, after that they could stay home and learn useful things like sewing and baking and washing and ironing. If they were rich enough to have servants, or slaves, they could learn to play the piano and sing a few tunes, and to paint china, and maybe even to read a bit of French, just to show that they were ladies and not just women!

Of course there were always a few girls who somehow broke through what Mary Lyon called "this empty gentility, this genteel nothingness," and showed that they had minds of their own. Some of them were lucky enough to have fathers who believed that girls had minds too—like that wonderful Margaret Fuller, whose father taught her Latin and Greek when she was hardly more than a baby, and who grew up in the company of artists and writers and philosophers and became something of an artist and a writer and a philosopher herself. Or like Elizabeth Cady for that matter. And some of them were just naturally so smart and so determined that nothing could stop them—not even the lack of an education.

Like Emma Willard, for example, or Mary Lyon, or Elizabeth Blackwell.

Here is Emma Willard, who had always longed for an education. But how did a New England country girl get herself an education? At last, after she was grown up and married, she had her chance. Her husband had moved to Middlebury, way up in northern Vermont, where he was in charge of an academy. Middlebury had a college too. Not for women, of course—don't be silly; there were no colleges for women. Everything was for men. But by great good luck Mrs. Willard had a nephew who was all ready for college, and off he went to Middlebury to get the education Mrs. Willard couldn't get. But there was nothing to prevent his aunt from reading all of his textbooks and learning all the things he learned—especially as she was smarter than he was. But what a way to get an education!

In 1814 Mrs. Willard thought that she had learned enough to teach on her own, and that year she opened a female seminary—that's what they were called then. It flourished, too; even the long, bitter winters couldn't freeze the desire for an education in the girls of Vermont. But Vermont was such a little state; Emma Willard needed a larger stage for her performance. One day she sat down and wrote a letter to Governor De Witt Clinton of the neighboring state of New York. What a famous letter that turned out to be. Governor Clinton was doing great things for education in New York; wouldn't he please try to do something for the education of girls while he was at it? High schools, seminaries, colleges—that was what Mrs. Willard proposed. It was a bold idea, but not too bold for the man who was to build the great Erie Canal three hundred miles across the state. Governor Clinton caught fire at once and sent off a message to the New York legislature with Mrs. Willard's proposals. And the legislature—well, it did nothing.

But all was not lost. For now some gentlemen in the city of Troy, New York, caught fire too. They invited Mrs. Willard to come to Troy and open a seminary there.

Within a year Emma Willard Seminary had opened its doors. The standards were high. It wasn't a college, but it acted as if it were. Latin, Greek, mathematics, science—all the hard subjects that young men studied at college. Quickly the word went out that here was a place where a clever girl could really get an education—not just in pouring tea and playing minuets on the piano and dancing the waltz. Soon girls were streaming in from all over the country to Mrs. Willard's seminary. For that matter they still are.

That was just the beginning for Emma Willard. With the seminary in full blast, she took off for Europe to study schools, to study them and to create them. It was a day when everybody was interested in Greece—which had had such a glorious past, and then long centuries of oppression, and which was now once again struggling for independence. The poet, Lord Byron, was out there fighting for the Greeks, and the "Chevalier" Samuel Gridley Howe. And Americans were naming their new towns Athens and Corinth and even Ypsilanti in honor of Greece; and all the new houses that went up had marble columns (or just wooden columns made to look like marble) in the Greek style. Mrs. Willard, too, wanted to help Greece. She couldn't fight, not with guns anyway, so she did what she could. She went to Athens and opened a school to train women teachers for

Greek schools. It was the first teacher-training school opened by any American—earlier even than Horace Mann's normal school in Lexington.

Mary Lyon aimed even higher. She wanted a real college for women—not just a finishing school or a seminary. She got it, too.

She usually got what she went after. Her father had died when she was scarcely more than a baby, and there had been little time for school, or money either. But Mary didn't really need time: she could learn twice as fast as anyone else, even in Yankee Massachusetts where babies were born with glasses on. Twice as fast? Why, ten times as fast is closer to the truth. She went through an English grammar in four days, learning it all by heart. Then she found a Latin grammar and mastered it in three days. Think of that next time you have to learn to decline a Latin verb over the weekend! She managed to get a bit of schooling at the Amherst Academy, and when she was fifteen she began to teach school herself. A little later she was teaching in her own academy over in Ipswich, north of Boston, next door to where Anne Hutchinson had set herself up as the equal of the Puritan minister . . . remember? And all the while Mary Lyon was dreaming of something better: a college for girls.

As yet there was no such thing in all America—or for that matter in all of England either. Imagine: nowhere could girls get a proper education! But already things were stirring. In 1835 Oberlin College, out in Ohio, opened its doors to women as well as to men. Wonderful little Oberlin, so full of courage and of ideas; two years later it welcomed Negroes too. It was the first college anywhere in the world to admit both women and Negroes. No wonder it grew to be one of the great colleges of the world, with that kind of beginning.

"When you have a great object in view let no obstacle,

no difficulty, distract you from it. Go where no one else is willing to go; do what no one else is willing to do." So wrote Mary Lyon, and she practiced what she preached. She had a great object in view: a college for women that should be as good as any college for men—as good as Harvard or Yale or Amherst in the lovely village where she had gone to school.

All through her years of teaching Mary Lyon talked about her college and planned for it and raised money for it. You could see her, flitting from town to town with her green velvet bag, talking in churches and in sewing circles and in schools, raising money for her college—five dollars here, two dollars there. It all went into the green bag, and in the end the green bag turned into a college. At last, in 1837, she was ready to start. She chose the village of South Hadley, in the Connecticut Valley, not far from Amherst, and named the college after one of the hills along the banks of the placid Connecticut River—Mount Holyoke College. It was a real college, too, not just a finishing school, its courses modeled on those at Amherst College, and some of the Amherst professors rode along the winding roads and over the notch in the hills to South Hadley to teach them. The Amherst professors weren't the only ones who rode over the notch, either; if any of you should go to Amherst College, or to Mount Holyoke, you will quickly discover how well worn is the road over the notch between the two colleges.

Now at last women had a college of their own. What an excitement on opening day, as fathers and mothers drove up with their daughters—real pioneers, those daughters—with Miss Lyon there to receive them and show them the red brick building rising up five stories high out of a muddy waste. What a glorious confusion. You could hear the carpenters hammering away, and there were workmen tacking down the carpets, and young ladies sitting around a table hemming the linen, and others scurrying around the kitchen getting up some kind of lunch for the hungry students and their parents. And teachers sitting on the stair steps giving examinations to the entering freshmen. . . . All new, and raw, but then so was Harvard College when it started, in 1636, and a little time would take care of all that. Everybody pitched in to help, those first years: the townspeople, and the parents and the girls, who brought flowers and shrubs from home to plant in the grounds, and even some of the young men from Amherst College. And how the girls clamored to get in! Why, the year after Mount Holyoke College opened Miss Lyon had to turn away four hundred of them.

Mary Lyon made two things so clear that they never had to be proved again.

One was that girls wanted to go to college, just like boys.

The other was that girls could learn anything that young men could learn.

Anything?

Yes, anything.

Look at Elizabeth Blackwell, who wanted to be a doctor.

Who ever heard of a *woman* doctor? Women weren't smart enough for doctoring. Women weren't strong enough to saw off arms and legs. Women would faint dead away if they saw blood.

And besides, it was immodest and indecent.

Then why did a nice young lady like Elizabeth Blackwell want to be a doctor?

Well, one reason was because she was told that she *couldn't,* and she wouldn't stand for that. She came from an independent family, did Elizabeth . . . from a family that knew its own mind and, what's more, had minds to know.

Her brother Henry believed so strongly in women's rights that he married Lucy Stone and together they spent all their lives crusading for women. . . . Who was Lucy Stone?

She was the young lady who saw no reason why she should give up her own name, just because she married, and so she kept her name. To this day married women who keep their own names are called Lucy Stoners.

And another brother, Dr. Samuel Blackwell, married Antoinette Brown, who was the first woman preacher in the country. She had gone to Oberlin College, of course—just like Lucy Stone. Once when Miss Brown went to a temperance convention the delegates spent the whole time arguing about whether or not she should be allowed to speak. The editor of the New York *Tribune*, the famous Horace Greeley, reported the convention this way:

First day: Crowding a woman off the platform.
Second day: Gagging her.
Third day: Voting that she shall stay gagged.

As if you could gag the Reverend Antoinette Brown Blackwell!

But let's get back to Elizabeth, wearing her heart out to be a doctor. It wasn't just that she was "contrary-minded," as they used to say in New England, and wanted to do what she wasn't allowed to do. Of course there was more to it than that. She wanted to do some good in the world. She wanted to help the poor and the sick, to relieve some of the pain and suffering that she saw all around her. And what better way to do that than to be a doctor?

She was teaching in the South when she made up her mind to study medicine, and the first thing she did was to persuade a professor at the College of Medicine down in Charleston to let her study his medical books. Even that was a pretty daring request from a young lady, and most doctors would simply have said no. But Professor Dickson was pretty daring himself, so he said yes.

Next, a medical school. But where?

There was not a medical school in the country that would take a woman. Elizabeth found that out all right when she started writing around to them: Harvard, Philadelphia, Jefferson, Louisville . . . No! No! No! No! always the same.

But wait. Here's one that says yes! It is the Geneva Medical School, up in New York, not far from Seneca Falls where Elizabeth Cady Stanton is busy drafting a Declaration of Independence.

They didn't really mean to admit her at the Geneva Medical School, but the professors put it up to the students, and the students thought, What a lark! A woman studying medicine; let's let her come and make a fool of herself.

So off she went, to Geneva. The professors didn't approve of her at all; the townspeople in Geneva said that she was "either mad or bad," but she stuck to it all the same, working twice as hard as any of the men. In the end she graduated at the head of her class. Then over to Europe for more study—to Paris, to Berlin, to the famous St. Bartholomew's Hospital in London. When she was through she knew lots more medicine than most other American doctors.

You'd think her troubles were at an end, but they had just begun. Back to New York came Elizabeth Blackwell, with high hopes, but she couldn't find an office and she couldn't get into a hospital, and she couldn't practice medicine. She opened a little clinic in the slums of New York where poor women could come for help, and after a while she bought a house down in what is now "the Village" and opened an infirmary for women, with all women doctors and nurses—that meant herself, her sister, and a poor Polish refugee woman.

A women's hospital, women doctors—how shocking! Whenever the hoodlums and toughs of that district couldn't think of anything better—or worse—to do, they would stand in front of Dr. Blackwell's hospital and sneer at her and at her patients and throw rocks through windows and show in many other ways how superior men were to women.

But Dr. Blackwell kept on, and won the affection of her patients and the respect of other doctors in the city. Then came the Civil War, with its terrible need for nurses, and Dr. Blackwell trained nurses for the army, and then went down to Washington to see that they got where they could do the most good. For the stuffed shirts in Washington had the curious notion that women shouldn't be allowed to be nurses—not unless they were very old or very plain, anyway. But they soon had to give up that notion, and thank their stars they could get nurses trained by people like Dr. Blackwell.

After the war things were different. The country was used to women nurses now; and no longer shocked at the idea of women doctors. In 1868 Dr. Blackwell was able to open not only a new women's infirmary but a medical school for women as well. What a triumph in twenty years!

Then Dr. Blackwell sailed back to England, where she had been born, and became a professor at the London School of Medicine, and for thirty years she trained women doctors, hundreds of them, who went out to all parts of the world. For by now women nurses and doctors were like women teachers: they were the most natural thing in the world. Nobody could remember when they didn't have women doctors. But Elizabeth Blackwell could.

Now we can go back to Elizabeth Stanton and Susan Anthony and their lifelong struggle to win votes for women.

They were very old by now, both of them in their eighties, but no matter. The torch that they carried will not fall to the ground or be snuffed out. There are always younger women to take it and hold it high.

Like Carrie Chapman Catt.

She really *was* young, too. When Mrs. Stanton wrote that Declaration of Independence, Carrie wasn't even born. When Susan Anthony got herself arrested for voting, Carrie was a little girl of thirteen with a pigtail and freckles.

It's difficult to tell you how different she was from Mrs.

Mott and Mrs. Stanton and Miss Anthony. She wasn't even a New Englander. She wasn't even a Quaker.

She was just a little girl who grew up on an Iowa farm and went to a country school, and when she was through with high school she said she was going to the state university—just like that. By now, though, that was no longer surprising; out west girls took it for granted that they could go to the state university just as boys did—especially in Iowa, which was the first state to admit girls to its university. . . . So Carrie taught school and saved her money and went off to the university, and learned not only history and literature but how to speak in public. When she was through she went back to teaching, and before she was twenty-five she was superintendent of schools at Mason City, which was a pretty big city as cities went out in Iowa in those days. She didn't stay superintendent very long, though; she got married instead, and then she got interested in politics and that meant that she got interested in votes for women. For what was the use of politics if you couldn't even vote?

You will remember that Elizabeth Stanton and Susan Anthony made a wonderful team. Well, Carrie Chapman Catt made a wonderful team too—all by herself. She could speak and write and get people excited, just like Mrs. Stanton; she could plan and organize and work behind the scenes, just like Miss Anthony. She had all the energy in the world, and after she married George Catt, who was a famous engineer, she had all the money she needed too, and she could give her time to the crusade for votes. There had been a kind of laying on of hands from Lucretia Mott to Elizabeth Stanton, and now there was another laying on of hands from old Susan Anthony to Mrs. Catt.

And now in 1900 the clouds were breaking up at last and the sun was streaming through. Even Miss Anthony, eighty-five years old, and intrepid to the last, could see that. "Mine eyes have seen the glory of the coming of the Lord," she sang in her cracked old voice, and it was true. Now nothing could stop the triumph of the great cause to which she had given her life. It was hard to believe that it was just the other day that it had all seemed so ridiculous, even so wicked. . . . One state after another gave the vote to women, and with the vote went all those other rights that they had fought for, so hard and so long.

Then came World War I. It was a war for democracy, said President Wilson, a war for democracy everywhere in the world. Then why not start at home? Why not start by giving the vote to women everywhere in the United States? That's democracy.

And that is just what happened. President Wilson spoke out for the rights of women, and in 1919 Congress passed the Nineteenth Amendment to the Constitution—you can remember it by all those nineteens—giving the vote to women everywhere.

Would the states agree? Most of them would, but some of them held back. Then up and down the country went Mrs. Catt, talking to legislatures and pleading with the public and meeting with governors and addressing meetings and writing letters, and one by one the states fell into line. Finally there was just Tennessee—it all seemed to hinge on that state. The fight went on for weeks and weeks. In the end it was decided by the youngest member of the legislature, Harry Burns—scarcely more than a boy. "Vote for suffrage," his mother wrote him. "Don't forget to be a good boy and *help Mrs. Catt.*" He did, too—and the amendment passed.

Weary but happy, Mrs. Catt came home to New York. When she got off the train in the Pennsylvania Station with the sun slanting down through the windows into the great hall, there was Governor Alfred E. Smith to greet her, in full dress, and a military band playing "Hail, the Conquering Hero Comes" and the streets black with men and women waving flags and throwing confetti and cheering themselves hoarse.

What a change since 1848. If only Lucretia Mott and Elizabeth Stanton and Susan Anthony could have lived to see it.

So women's rights won out in the end, just as the crusade for freedom for the Negro won out, just as the crusade for the rights of children won out. Who would have thought it? Who would have thought it when Lucretia Mott was forced off the platform at the London convention? Who would have thought it when the Seneca Falls convention passed that ridiculous resolution about votes for women? Who would have thought it when Mary Lyon opened her struggling little college in the hills of New England? Who would have thought it when rowdies smashed up Dr. Blackwell's shabby little infirmary down in New York?

Remember:

*One man with a dream, at pleasure,*
*Shall go forth and conquer a crown;*
*And three with a new song's measure*
*Can trample an empire down.*

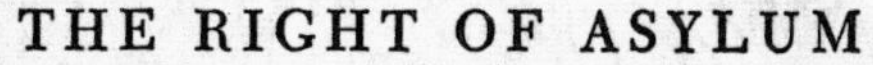

# THE RIGHT OF ASYLUM

JULY
IV

Asylum. It is a Greek word. It means, quite simply, security. It means a place where you are safe—like home.

Remember the Pilgrims who took refuge in the Dutch city of Leyden, and then sailed on the *Mayflower* to the sandy shores of Cape Cod? Remember the Puritans, twenty shiploads of them, crossing the stormy seas to Boston Harbor and setting up the Massachusetts Bay Colony? Remember Roger Williams fleeing across the winter snows to the islands of Narragansett Bay and setting up the colony of Rhode Island where everybody was allowed to worship as he pleased? . . . And William Penn bringing over thousands of Quakers from England and Lutherans from the Rhine Valley to his colony of Pennsylvania?

All of them fleeing from persecution or injustice or war. All of them finding *asylum* in the New World.

It is an old story, the story of flight and asylum—and a story that is ever fresh and new. It is as old as the Jews wandering for forty years in the Wilderness, seeking the

Promised Land, and as new as the story of refugees trying to escape from Communist East Germany to Republican West Germany.

People in flight! Thousands and thousands of them, sometimes millions of them. Swarming onto the roads, fording rivers and crossing mountains, crowding into little cockle-shell boats, fleeing before the men on horseback with their long spears, or before the men in armor with their muskets, or the men in tanks with their guns, or the men in airplanes circling overhead and dropping bombs on the helpless refugees below.

Men and women in flight, giving up everything—their homes, their farms, their cattle, the flowers they had planted in the garden, the furniture they had made, the books and pictures they had learned to love, the toys and dolls they had played with. Giving up everything—their towns and villages, their neighbors, their schools, their churches, their life work . . . hoping to find asylum in some new land.

Why can't people live together in peace? Why must those who win wars drive out those who lose? Surely there is room enough for all of them?

Why must those of one race or one color drive out those of another race or another color?

Why must those who worship God one way drive out those who worship Him in a different way?

Look at France under Louis XIV, who sat on the throne for sixty-five years—all the time from 1660 to 1715. That's a long time to be King.

He was called the Sun King. He was the sun around which all lesser stars revolved. He was the sun, and all light streamed out from him. If he was not there, all was dark.

Anyway, that's what he thought.

Naturally, he thought that everything should be done

*his* way. When he stood up everybody should stand up. When he sat down everybody should stand up too, for that matter. When he took snuff everybody should sneeze.

One thing he was sure of. Everybody in France should worship just as he worshiped. He was a Catholic, so everybody should be a Catholic.

But everybody wasn't a Catholic in the France of his day. There were probably a million Protestants in France. They were called Huguenots—the word means "people who associate together"; we would probably call them Joiners. They had their own church, and their own pastors, and their own schools; they had their own way of life.

That was what Louis XIV couldn't stand—that anyone should have a religion or a way of life that was different from his.

In 1685 the blow fell. That year the Sun King made one of the worst mistakes in history. Of course he didn't admit that it was a mistake; a King can never make a mistake. But it was, all the same. For he said, "No more Protestants in France! Everybody has to have the same religion as the King." So all over France soldiers moved in on the families of the Huguenots. They settled on them, four or five soldiers to a household, and literally ate the people out of house and home. They beat the men and terrified the women and took the children away and put them in monasteries or nunneries. They closed Huguenot schools and churches and arrested Huguenot teachers and preachers.

What should the Huguenots do? What could they do but give in—or escape?

Then came the great flight of the Huguenots. From every village and town of France they streamed out toward the frontiers of neighboring countries. Picture them: old men with white beards, young mothers with babies in their arms, boys and girls tagging along behind their parents, here and there a young man driving a wagon loaded with blankets and food and a few bundles of clothing, and perhaps some old grandmother or sick child lying on the bundles. They traveled by night and hid by day, in the country barns or in patches of forest, for the King did not want them to leave the country and his soldiers had orders to stop them and arrest them if they tried to do so.

Some of them got over the border to nearby Holland. Others crossed the Rhine River into Germany. Others somehow fought their way across the mountains and reached the Swiss cantons. Still others, from the northern provinces, made their way to harbor cities like Brest or Le Havre and managed to hire little fishing boats to ferry them across the Channel to England, or perhaps hid away on some merchant vessel that sailed for more distant ports.

Altogether about three hundred thousand Huguenots left France and found asylum in other lands. That may not seem a great many to you, but imagine what it would be like if about three million Americans should leave the United States all at once.

How lucky that the Huguenots had somewhere to go.

Holland welcomed them, little Holland which had welcomed the Pilgrims, and which was one of the freest countries in the world. And thousands of Huguenots settled down in Amsterdam and Leyden and The Hague.

The cities of Switzerland welcomed them—Geneva by its lovely lake, and Berne in the middle of the Alps, and Basle at the head of the Rhine River—welcomed them and fed them and clothed them and cared for their sick, and kept as many of them as they could. Louis XIV threatened the Swiss with the most awful punishments for helping the Huguenots, but they refused to be afraid.

The German states welcomed them, especially Prussia, whose King collected money for them and gave them homes to live in.

Most important of all England welcomed them, raised money for them, let them set up their own churches and schools, and made them feel at home.

How fortunate for the Huguenots that they had other countries they could go to. But how fortunate for the other countries, too, that the Huguenots came.

France never quite got over losing three hundred thousand of her most intelligent and courageous inhabitants.

And the other countries never got over their good fortune in having so many Huguenots come to join them and be part of them.

Take America, for instance.

Nature, you might say, had made America an asylum—all that land, more than in the whole of Europe. But even in America there were some who said, "Stay out." Even here there were some who said, "You must speak *our* language, you must be of *our* race, you must worship *our* God, or we won't let you in."

That's what the Spaniards said, and they owned most of South America and a good part of North America too. They wouldn't let anyone in who wasn't both Spanish and Catholic. That's what the French said, and they owned all of Canada, and a good part of the Mississippi Valley as well. They wouldn't let anyone in who wasn't both French and Catholic.

But that's not what the English said. They sang a different tune. They didn't *quite* say, "Come one, come all," but that's really what it amounted to. So far as the English were concerned there was room enough for all, if not in one colony, then in another: if not in Massachusetts, then in Rhode Island; if not in New York, then in Pennsylvania; if not in Virginia, than in Carolina. Room for Pilgrims and Puritans, room for Quakers and Baptists, room for Catholics and Jews. And room for Huguenots.

Room? Why, everybody wanted the Huguenots. The Americans had that much sense anyway. Everybody wanted them, and they went everywhere. There weren't actually so many of them—perhaps fifteen or twenty thousand altogether—not as many people as go to a big college football game today. But what a difference they made! They scattered all through the English colonies—Massachusetts, New York, Virginia, South Carolina—and wherever they went they took with them their energy and industry, their courage and independence.

What a difference they made, these Huguenots from France. In no time at all they had made their mark in the new country, and in history too. Here is Peter Faneuil of Boston; his father fled to Holland, and then came to the Bay Colony, and now Peter has made a fortune and built the great hall that bears his name and given it to the people of Boston, and for them it became "the cradle of Liberty" —the hall where the men of Boston voted their colony into the Revolution. Or here is Apollos de Revoire; his son was that Paul Revere who made the famous midnight ride through the countryside, shouting that the British were coming—you remember him from Longfellow's poem. . . . Or here are the Bowdoins—one of them ended up as governor of Massachusetts and gave his name to a famous college —maybe you will go there someday, and be a poet like Henry Wadsworth Longfellow, who went there and who was part Huguenot too.

Or look at New York City and the nearby town of New Rochelle, named after old Rochelle on the coast of France. There had always been some Huguenots in New York, even when it was New Amsterdam—Peter Minuit, for example, the man who bought Manhattan Island from the Indians; or Judith Bayard, the wife of that Peter Stuyvesant who hobbled around on his wooden leg. Now came many more —the Jays for example; one of them was to be the first Chief Justice of the United States. Or the Bayards, who gave so many senators and diplomats to the United States. Or the De la Noyes. You may think you don't know them but remember Franklin *Delano* Roosevelt, and you will see that you do.

So it went everywhere in the colonies. Look at the Huguenots in the middle colonies, and think of Philip Freneau in New Jersey, who was the first real American poet, or the Du Ponts of Maryland with their gunpowder factory. And down in Charleston, South Carolina, every other name, it seemed, was Huguenot—and still is: Legaré and Manigault and Ravenel and Petigru and Laurens—who was Washington's friend—and General Francis Marion, who is remembered as the Swamp Fox of the Revolution.

France has done many good things for America: sending over Lafayette to help win independence is what you probably know best. But the best thing France ever did for America was something she had no notion of doing at all. It was sending so many Huguenots over to the New World.

We learned early, here in America, that it is a good thing to be an asylum.

That, in any event, is what America became: an asylum for those people of all countries who never had quite enough to eat; for those who weren't allowed to worship their own way; for those who were tired of soldiering, and of wars not of their making; for those who wanted to escape from the iron rule of emperors and dictators; for those who were despised and mistreated; for those who hungered and thirsted after an education, if not for themselves, then for their children.

A hundred years ago—oh, more than that even—there was a popular song that they knew even in Europe. It went like this:

*We have room for all creation, and our banner is unfurled,*
*Here's a general invitation to the people of the world:*
*Come along, come along, make no delay!*
*Come from every nation, come from every way!*
*Our lands are broad enough, don't be alarmed,*
*And Uncle Sam is rich enough to give us all a farm.*

And how they came, from every country of the Old World, shipload after shipload, pouring into New York Harbor, and Boston, and Baltimore, and New Orleans, too, and spreading out all over the country. Hundreds of thousands of Irish fleeing from starvation as from a pestilence: imagine starvation in that beautiful island. Germans—first a trickle of refugees from the Revolution of 1848 that didn't come off—the Forty-Eighters, they were called—and then a million others who fled from hunger and misery and war. They swarmed into Ohio and Wisconsin and Missouri until you would have thought that these were all German States, but pretty soon you couldn't tell them from the Yankees or the Irish or the Norwegians who had settled down in these states as well.

Then, later on, the Italians and the Poles and the Bohemians, coming to the land of a second chance. And the Jews from the ghettos of Poland and Russia, fleeing from bitter persecution and hoping to find an asylum where they would be treated as equals. And still later the refugees from the Russian Revolution, and the peoples from the little Baltic countries that Russia had swallowed up, and the Hungarians who fled from the iron grip of the Communists after they had tried a revolution and lost.

What a long story of poverty and misery and persecution. What a long story of asylum.

In 1876 France gave a birthday present to the United States, which was just one hundred years old: the present didn't actually arrive for another ten years, but that didn't matter. She gave the United States the Statue of Liberty which stands in the entrance of the harbor of New York, with its torch ever bright: it is the first thing everyone goes to see when he comes to New York. What did the Statue of Liberty stand for? The winning of independence by the Americans in 1776? Liberty for Americans? The friendship of America and France?

Yes, all of these. But most important was something else. The sculptor who made the statue—he was a Frenchman named Frédéric Bartholdi—called it Liberty Enlightening the World. Liberty was to stand in the harbor holding out the hand of welcome to all newcomers, and her flaming torch was to be the promise of freedom to them—to all of them. That is what Emma Lazarus saw. She was a New York Jewish girl who knew all about the suffering of her people in Russia and Poland and who had worked with the Jewish refugees who came flocking into New York. In 1886 she wrote a poem to be engraved on the pedestal of the Statue of Liberty:

*Here at our sea-washed, sunset gates shall stand*
*A mighty woman with a torch whose flame*
*Is the imprisoned lightning, and her name,*
*Mother of Exiles. From her beacon-hand*
*Glows world-wide welcome; her mild eyes command*
*The air-bridged harbor that twin cities frame.*
*"Keep, ancient lands, your storied pomp," cries she*
*With silent lips. "Give me your tired, your poor,*
*Your huddled masses yearning to breathe free,*
*The wretched refuse of your teeming shore,*
*Send these, the homeless, tempest-tossed, to me:*
*I lift my lamp beside the golden door."*

The tired, the poor, the huddled masses yearning to breathe free—those are the ones who found asylum in America.

America itself was an asylum, but the greatest champion of the right of asylum was not an American but a Norwegian. His name was Fridtjof Nansen.

Norway is just a little country, all mountains and snow and long winding fjords that cut deep into the coast, and with fewer people than half a dozen American cities today, but she has produced far more than her share of great men. None was greater than Fridtjof Nansen.

He even looked like a great man, and you don't know how unusual that is. Six feet tall, broad-shouldered, straight as a Norwegian pine, fierce blue eyes, golden hair—he looked like a Viking warrior, and he was. Even as an old man he was magnificent; at the League of Nations, in Geneva, they said that next to Mount Blanc the most splendid sight in all Switzerland was Fridtjof Nansen. They said that when he went by, even the mountains bowed down to him.

What a life of adventure and of peril; what a life of conquest—but always in the cause of peace. From the time he was a boy he had hurled himself against nature, steeled his body and his mind—but never his heart—against hardship. Before he was twenty he had crossed the towering mountains of Norway on skis—the first man ever to do that. Before he was twenty, too, he proved himself the fastest ice skater in the world. He could sail his boat on the Norwegian fjords in any weather; he could swim through the icy waters of the arctic seas; he could fight polar bears and wolves with only a hunting knife. And it wasn't all just strength and courage either: he could dissect a fish; he could test the currents of the polar seas, he could write books on icebergs, he could direct scientific expeditions and lecture at universities.

It was the arctic North that fascinated him—the only part of the world that had not yet been conquered. So he set out to conquer it. With three companions he did what had never been done before (unless by some unknown Eskimo)—he crossed the heart of the immense island of Greenland by sled and snowshoe and ski. Then, a few years later, he was off to chart the waters of the northern seas and to find the North Pole. He fitted out a ship—it was called the *Forward*—with food and medicines and supplies and a thousand books; he sailed it deep into arctic waters, drifting with the ice; then with a single companion he set out with skis and dog sleds to the North Pole, four hundred miles away. He didn't quite make it, but he came closer than anyone had ever come before. And he had lots of time to think, too, for the two men spent almost a year in an ice house—polar bear and walrus for food, bearskins for beds and blankets, blubber for light—before they managed to find their way back to their ship. When the *Forward* came sailing back into Oslo Harbor one September morning there were a hundred ships out to greet it, and cannon booming from the forts, and the flags fluttering from every house, and the waterfront black with people to welcome Nansen home.

It was not just that he had reached farthest north. That stirred everybody's imagination, to be sure—that and the story of courage. But there was more to it than that. It had been a great scientific expedition as well, and in the end it took six big volumes to tell the story of all the scientific findings. No wonder his own university made him a professor, and universities all over the world hastened to honor him.

A great sportsman; a great explorer; a great writer; a great scientist.

That was enough of a career for any man.

But wait! We have hardly begun.

> "The peaks have been reached, they were so low. The vast expanse seems small and the snow fields no longer gleam, the mountain tarn is not high nor lonely and the white swans are flown. But once more, yet once more, the wings can be stretched for one flight beyond the peaks and the glaciers, O brave dreamer!"

That's what Nansen himself said, and that is the best description of him: brave dreamer.

First there were years of quiet teaching at the university, and writing scientific books, and then years of politics and diplomacy. In 1905 Norway separated from Sweden. Most separations cause wars; it was Nansen who helped make certain that this would be a peaceful separation. His wife was alarmed that Norway might set up as a republic, for she was sure that if it did the Norwegian people would make Nansen their first President. That's just what they would have done, too. Nansen himself thought that a King would be better—a King was what they had always been used to. So he went over to Denmark and persuaded a Danish Prince to become King of Norway, and then went home and persuaded the Norwegian people that they really wanted a King and not a President.

Now came a new career. "All my life I have been waiting for the great idea to which my life was to be engaged," Nansen said. It was not the conquest of the North Pole—nor yet of the South Pole, which for a time he planned. It was the conquest of hunger and persecution and wrong. It was saving the victims of war. It was finding asylum for the refugees of the whole world.

In 1914 Europe was plunged into war, and for four years the main business of almost every country was killing and burning and destroying. Great armies swarmed through the countryside battering down cities and wiping out villages, looting homes and factories, libraries and museums, tearing up railroad tracks and breaking down bridges, killing off cattle and poultry, and trampling down the grain in the fields. Everywhere they went they left an ocean of ruins. Then at last the guns fell silent and the armies ceased to march. But the ruins were there, and the misery and poverty and hunger lingered on for years. Millions of men had been killed and other millions were in prison camps. Millions of men and women and children had lost their homes and were face to face with starvation.

To Fridtjof Nansen—as to Jane Addams in America—it was all madness. What was Europe about, destroying itself in this way? What were human beings about? Even animals didn't kill off their own kind. At the end of the war Nansen threw all of his energies into helping Woodrow Wilson create the new League of Nations. The League, they hoped, would find a way to heal the wounds of war and to prevent future wars.

If the American President Woodrow Wilson was the man who did most to create the League of Nations, it was Nansen who did most to make it useful.

By now Nansen was one of the three or four great citizens of the world. As soon as the war was over, one problem after another was dumped into his lap. Each one was more than any one man could possibly solve, but Nansen took them all and did the best he could with each of them.

First they asked him to take charge of the job of getting prisoners of war back to their own countries. Above all, the German prisoners, who were in camps in faraway Siberia, and the Russian prisoners, who were in camps in Germany —altogether half a million of them. Everything had to be done from the beginning. First Nansen had to get the countries to agree to the return of their prisoners. Then he had to find the ships and the railroad trains to take them home. He had to feed them on the way, set up camps to receive them, vaccinate them and bring the sick ones back to health, find new homes for them if they had lost their old homes. It was an immense job, but Nansen wound it up in two years.

Somehow it ran into another and even harder job. That was taking care of over a million refugees.

Most of them were refugees from Russia, for Russia had gone through not only a war but a revolution, and you know what happens during a revolution. There are always some who oppose a revolution, and when the revolutionists win, the opposers are the ones who have to run for their lives. It had happened many times before in history; even in America the Tories who opposed the Revolution had to flee to Canada, sixty or seventy thousand of them. Now there were a million Russians, scattered all over Europe and Asia too—all the way from France to China. Most of them wanted to get home again. But how to bring them home? They were really lost, these refugees: no money, no jobs, not even a country to belong to, for their old country—the Russia of Tsar Nicholas—was gone, and as yet they hadn't found a new country. Nansen took charge of everything. He rounded up the refugees, put them on ships and on trains, and sent them back to their homeland. He supplied them with food and clothing and medicine. He even gave them special passports—the famous Nansen passports: every country in the world would accept the name "Nansen" even if it wouldn't accept any other name. Within a few years Nansen had returned over a million refugees to their own homes.

Then on top of that came the terrible problem of the Greek refugees—again almost a million of them. For centuries they had lived in that broad mountainous land we call Asia Minor—in Anatolia and Smyrna. Now the Turks wanted that land for themselves, and they drove out the Greeks. How would they get back to Greece? Who would feed them as they crowded along the dusty roads; who would take care of those too weak to walk; who would take care of them when they finally arrived back on Greek soil? Greece couldn't do it—she had suffered through the war just like so many other countries. The Turks wouldn't do it: "Not our responsibility," they said. The answer was Nansen. Always Nansen. Nansen would raise the money. Nansen would find the ships and send the food. Nansen would round up the doctors and the nurses to take care of the sick. Nansen would persuade the governments to bestir themselves—to set aside land, to find work for the newcomers, to set up hospitals and schools. And of course Nansen did.

And while he was busy with the problem of taking care

of the Greek refugees another and even more terrible problem was given him to solve.

Remember the Four Horsemen of the Apocalypse: War, Famine, Pestilence, and Death? Now all four of them rode down the Russians. First the war—and they had been defeated in war. Then the Revolution. And after that, Famine and Pestilence and, of course, Death. Death not of thousands but of millions. For there was a terrible drought all through the Ukraine and the great valley of the Volga—it was as if the whole Mississippi Valley from Pittsburgh to Kansas City should go through a year without water. The crops withered on the ground; the cattle died of thirst. Twenty million people were threatened with starvation. Then pestilence swept the stricken land, cholera and typhus. Poor Russia!

What to do? There was plenty of food in the world—in the United States or in the Argentine or off in Australia. There were plenty of ships on the Atlantic. There were even plenty of men who had no work and would have been glad to pitch in and help. How bring all these together—the food and the ships and the men—and use them to save the starving Russians?

Again the League of Nations put the job on Nansen. Could he bring help in time? He turned to his old friend Herbert Hoover, in America—the man who had brought food to the starving Belgians even during the war: there never was a better man for organizing things than Herbert Hoover. Between them they raised almost one hundred million dollars, bought food, chartered the ships and the trains, broke through all the tangles of red tape, and somehow got food over to Russia. Not enough, to be sure—four million Russians starved to death that winter of 1921. But millions who might have starved were saved.

Now, after the war, one more task, the most heartbreaking of all, was put on the broad shoulders of old Fridtjof

Nansen: the task of finding asylum for still another stricken people. This time it was the Armenians, an ancient Christian people who for centuries had lived in the midst of the Moslem peoples of the East. For centuries, too, they had been persecuted by the Turks—their priests killed, their churches burned, their people driven from one region to another. Now, with the war going on, the Turks were resolved to put an end to the Armenians. The method was simple: kill them off. Men, women, children—it made no difference. Altogether in these years the Turkish tyrant Mustafa Kemal killed over one third of all the Armenian people. Somehow the others managed to escape, thousands of them to Greece, other thousands to Syria on the Mediterranean, but most of them to the new Armenian state deep in the Caucasus Mountains which is now a part of Soviet Russia.

But meantime they had to be saved. They were without food and clothing, without tools for farming or for work; without medicines or doctors or nurses. Could anything be done for them? Could enough of them be saved to start a new Armenian nation? Once again it was up to Dr. Nansen. Nansen appealed to the whole world and the world responded. Money and supplies poured in, and somehow Nansen managed to get most of it out to the stricken Armenian refugees. He brought in the food and the medicine, and shipped in the machines and tools so that they could get started again. And in time they built up a new flourishing Armenia.

Not long before he died Nansen was elected rector of the ancient University of St. Andrews in Scotland. It was an honor that the young men voted him, and he went over to them and made a speech. When he spoke he spoke to all who were young—to all who are ever young—even to you:

> What a joyous thing to see the day dawning and to know that you are bound on a voyage to new realms. Your soul bounds upwards on beams of light to the vault of heaven. You laugh at the risks and smile at the dangers. Youth's buoyant faith and self-trust is in command.

All his life Fridtjof Nansen was on voyages to new realms—new realms of physical discovery, new realms of work, new realms of faith. He was the greatest of all explorers because he explored not only the face of the globe but the hearts of mankind.

You have met a good many heroes in this book—men like Roger Williams and Tom Paine and Sarmiento and James Yen. Now meet a country that is a hero: Israel.

Like America, it is an *asylum*.

It was easy for America to be an asylum. All that land—as Thomas Jefferson said, "Land enough for our descendants to the thousandth and thousandth generation"—and most of it empty. All the wealth of soil and forest and river, of coal and iron and oil. No wonder Americans could sing, "We have room for all creation." They had, too.

But now look at Israel. It is just a little country, wedged in between all those other countries on the eastern shore of the Mediterranean Sea, so little you can hardly find it. Why, you could tuck it away in a corner of Texas or California and scarcely know it was there. And if you do find it, and look at it closely, you will see that most of it is desert.

If the American song was "Come along, come along, make no delay" you might almost suppose that the song of Israel would be taken from the Mad Hatter's tea party—remember? "No room, no room."

But it turned out just the other way around.

In modern times—in the last thirty years, that is—the United States has begun to worry about having enough room, and has got very choosy about whom it will allow to come in. A few thousand here, a few thousand there; not more than two or three hundred thousand newcomers each year. For a country like the United States that's nothing; why, more than ten times that many babies are born each year.

It was little Israel that said, "Come one, come all."

Have you ever heard of the Wandering Jew? He is a character out of the world of fiction: an old Jew who is doomed to live forever, and whose fate it is always to be wandering from country to country, never at rest or at peace.

He is not entirely a character out of fiction, though. He is a symbol of the Jewish people. Over two thousand years ago the Jews were driven out of their home in Palestine—they called it Israel—and they scattered to every quarter of the globe. You found Jews in northern Africa, in Spain and Portugal, in Germany and Poland and Russia, in Persia and India and even in distant China. Wherever you went you would find a Jewish community. And if you could look into the minds and hearts of the members of those communities, you would see that many of them longed to return to Israel.

Every Sabbath day they would sit in their temples and say, with their rabbis, "If I forget Thee, O Jerusalem, let my right hand forget its cunning. May my tongue cleave to my palate if I remember you not, if I place not Jerusalem ahead of my joy."

No wonder so many of them wanted to return to Israel. Almost everywhere in the world they were mistreated and persecuted. Not for any fault of theirs, not for any wrongs that they had done, not because they were not good citizens. No, simply because they were Jews.

They were herded into the slums of great cities—slums

called ghettos. They were made to wear special clothes with markings that told that they were Jews. They were not allowed to work at the jobs that they could do best, or enter the professions, but were given jobs that no one else wanted. They were not allowed to go to schools or universities, or vote, or hold office. They were not even second-class citizens; they weren't citizens at all.

They could endure most of that. They could live in their ghettos and make a living at trades like tailoring; they could even manage without schools because they had their own schools and their own learned men.

What made their lot too hard to bear was persecution. Whenever things went wrong—when times were hard, when there was poverty, or a defeat, or a plague—the people took it out on the Jews. In city after city, in country after country, mobs would run riot and attack the ghettos. They would break into the temples, drag the rabbis through the streets, sack the ghettos, kill all who resisted. Sometimes it wasn't just the mobs—it was the King, whose soldiers swarmed into the Jewish quarters and cut down all who got in their way.

Not a nice story, this story of the persecution of the Jews by the Christians.

And it wasn't just something that happened a long time ago, either—like the persecution of the Huguenots in France. It was something that went right on, year after year, down to our own time.

How did the Jews survive? They survived by holding fast to their religion and making it the cement that bound them together. They survived by their love of learning, and by teaching to each new generation of children the history of Israel and of its religion.

And in the bad years of the late 1800s they survived by finding asylum in the United States: thousands and thousands of them, crowding into the steerage of ships and sailing over to New York and its Statue of Liberty.

And they survived, too, on hopes and on dreams—the hope of returning someday to their homeland; the dream of making Israel once again a real nation.

They almost didn't survive at all. Just a few years ago—so recently your parents can tell you about it—the Jews were the victims of the worst tragedy that ever happened to any people since the time five hundred years ago when the Spanish conquerors wiped out the Indians of Mexico and Peru.

In 1932 Adolf Hitler seized power in Germany and began his career of crime. If there has ever been a more wicked man in history, it is hard to think who it could have been. Everything that Hitler did was wicked, but the most wicked thing that he did was to try to kill off all the Jews—not only the Jews of Germany but of every country that he conquered. He almost succeeded, too, in this awful ambition. During the years that he was absolute dictator of Germany—and of Austria and Poland and France and many other helpless nations—he killed almost every Jew in all of those countries. Altogether Hitler killed almost six million Jews.

A few escaped. Some of them managed to hide. Some of them managed to escape to countries like Sweden and Switzerland which were not in the war and could give them asylum. Some of them managed to get over to America—great scientists like Albert Einstein and great writers like Thomas Mann. And a few managed to survive the terrible camps where they were imprisoned and waiting for death.

Even before the war, some Jews had been encouraged to go back to Israel to live. Now, when Hitler was at last defeated and the war was over, the word went out to all the Jews who still survived that they could find asylum in Israel. Come home to Israel. Come from every land, come from every continent, come and build up the ancient home of the Jewish people! And Israel passed a law called the

Law of the Return, which made every newcomer a citizen of Israel the moment he set foot in the country.

Then began one of the great stories of history, the "ingathering" of the exiles. From every quarter of the globe Jewish people streamed into the little country hugging the shore of the blue Mediterranean. They came from the prison camps of Germany and Poland, from the rubble of cities that had been leveled to the ground, from the ghettos of Russia and Rumania. They came from the ancient states of North Africa—Egypt and Morocco and Algiers—and from the even more ancient countries of Asia—Persia and India and China. They came, some of them, from England and France and the United States, not to escape persecution—for there were no persecutions in these countries—but to have a part in the great adventure of building a new nation.

On they came, year after year, the young and the old, the lame and the blind, those who had been beggared and those who had suffered from persecution. They came afoot, they came by ship, they even came by plane. The ancient Yemenite peoples, tucked away in the deserts of Arabia, heard of the new homeland and began to walk across the desert, hoping to get to Israel. Soon they were stranded and faced with starvation. Their religion told them that one day they should be borne on the wings of an eagle to the Promised Land, and lo, airplanes swooped down out of the skies and picked them up and carried them all to Israel, fifty thousand of them, just as had been prophesied.

On they came, year after year, streaming in to this tiny plot of ground. The Arabs tried to stop them, and they had to fight for their life. They lost half of their ancient capital, Jerusalem, and they built a new Jerusalem. The old cities had fallen into ruins and they built new cities. There wasn't enough land to go around, and they turned desert land into farm land. Their people were poor and sick and ignorant and they gave them work, and cured them, and sent them to school.

In ten years little Israel gave asylum to more than one million Jews. They planted olive trees and orange and lemon trees in the soft hills along the Sea of Galilee, and brought water down from the river Jordan to give life to the soil and cover the brown hills with a coat of green. They built little farming villages out on the edge of the desert and grew enough food for their needs. They moved into the great desert of the south called the Negev, and brought water into it and made it bloom like the rose.

In ten years they made a new nation—one of the smallest nations in the world and one of the greatest nations in the world.

The United States and Israel: two asylums that became nations, two nations that became asylums.

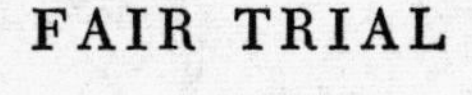

# FAIR TRIAL

Duty, Honor, Reverence, Loyalty—those are great words, and they have a great history. We couldn't do without them. We certainly couldn't tell the story of human rights without them.

But they are not words that *you* use very often.

There is another word that means more to you than any of these—certainly one that you use oftener than you use any of these.

It is "fair."

Fair play. That's the only kind of play that is possible. Not to play fair is cheating, and you can't play at all if there is cheating.

Fair fight. That's the one condition of any fight—that it should be clean and fair. The two words mean the same thing. Not to fight fair—well, Americans call it "hitting below the belt"; the English say, "That's not cricket." It means the same thing; it's dirty.

Fair shares. You don't want more than your share, and

you don't want others to have more than their share either. To take more than your share is being a pig.

"No fair!" It is the cry of children all over the world. It is a universal word. No fair looking when you are "it" in a game of hide-and-seek. No fair getting a head start in a race. No fair getting your father or mother to help you in a contest that is supposed to be for children. No fair looking at the cards when you play solitaire. No fair having an extra player on your team. . . . No fair! When you've said that, you've said everything.

Without fair play nothing works; certainly nothing is any fun. You can't have any games without fair play. You can't run a school without fair play. Even a family can't get along together unless there is fair play.

Without fair trial nothing works either.

What fair play is to the world of children, fair trial is to the world of grown people. Just as you play your games according to the rules, and have an umpire to make decisions and enforce the rules, so the grown-up world runs its business according to rules. They are the rules of law. And it has umpires to make decisions and enforce them. They are judges and courts.

If your teams don't play according to the rules or if your umpires should call all the decisions on one side, the game breaks down. And if the affairs of men are not conducted according to the rules of law or if judges give all the decisions on one side, everything breaks down too. When men and women have to cry, "No fair!" confidence is gone—confidence in the law and the courts and the government. Then pretty soon society itself starts to come apart at the seams.

Fair play—fair trial: they mean pretty much the same thing and they work the same way. Fair play for the poor as for the rich; for the ignorant as for the learned; for the weak as for the strong. Fair play for Protestants in Catholic countries and for Catholics in Protestant countries, and for Jews in all countries, and even for those who haven't any religion at all. Fair play for Negroes as for whites; fair play for peasants as for lords, for workingmen as for merchant princes. Fair play for those who are "otherwise minded" as well as for those who hold all the popular ideas and agree with everybody about everything. Fair play for those who are wrong as well as for those who are right.

Fair play means that nobody is above the law and nobody is below the law. Nobody is so great or so powerful that the law cannot speak up and say "Stop!" Nobody is so poor and helpless that the law cannot look down and find him and protect him.

The law!

We have read about a good many discoveries and inventions in this book. Did you ever think what a wonderful invention the law is? The law says what is right and what is wrong. It says what is just and what is unjust. It sets up governments and says how they are to be run. It arranges for marriages and for the duties of parents and of children to each other. It fixes the hours of work, and protects women and children against overwork. It sets up schools and colleges and libraries. It controls airplanes and railroads and automobiles. It inspects food and water and protects your health. It builds playgrounds and hospitals.

What does it not do!

But whatever it does, it has to be fair.

"Freedom," said a great English philosopher, "is a standing law to live by." Think of that: freedom is law.

It's really a very old idea, this idea of fair play and fair trial. You can find it in the Old Testament, and in the histories of Greece and Rome. The trouble is that for hundreds of years men said, "Yes, what a wonderful idea!" and then didn't pay any attention to it, just as they say, "Peace!

What a wonderful idea," and then go out and start another war.

We can say just when and where the idea of fair trial began to loom up as really important. It was in June of the year 1215, in England. To be exact, at a field called Runnymede, on an island in the Thames River outside the city of London. For that was the year that two thousand knights and barons met with King John of England and complained of all their hardships, and said that they would no longer pay taxes to him or fight for him unless he agreed to give them their rights. Those rights were written down in what is called Magna Carta, or the Great Charter. And King John signed it, all right; he had no choice in the matter.

There were a good many rights set forth in the Great Charter, but only one of them concerns us. It is number 39. What did it say?

> No free man shall be imprisoned or outlawed or banished or in any way molested . . . except by the lawful judgment of his peers and by the law of the land.

There it is. Nobody arrested or put in prison, except by the law of the land.

Not by a King, pounding the table and roaring, "Off with his head!"

Not by soldiers bursting into a man's house and seizing him and carrying him off to the Tower of London, or to the Bastille in Paris, or to any dungeon.

Not by a judge saying, "I am the law," and hurrying some poor wretch off to the gallows.

No. By the law of the land. By fair trial. By a jury picked from the plain people of the neighborhood.

Of course it didn't happen all at once. Kings continued to pound tables and say, "Off with his head." Soldiers smashed their way into houses and hauled their victims off to prison. Judges went on thinking that they were the law, or making up the law as they went along.

But all the time there was that promise in the Great Charter: the law of the land; fair trial.

And gradually, over the years, it loomed up larger and larger until finally nobody dared ignore it, not even kings or soldiers or judges.

What did it mean? Or perhaps we should ask, what meanings clustered around it and attached themselves to it and became part of it—just as meanings cluster around a person and become part of him when we know him better?

It meant that everybody, high and low, had a right to fair play. It meant that you couldn't be arrested by soldiers or by the police without good cause. You couldn't be clamped in jail and allowed to rot there, forgotten by everybody except your own family. You couldn't be tortured to make you confess to things that you hadn't done. You had a right to a fair trial: to a judge who was fair, and a jury who were fair, and witnesses who were fair. If anybody lied about you, you could challenge him. You could tell your own story, your own way. You had a right to a lawyer to help you. You were innocent until the Court proved you guilty. And even if you were guilty you still couldn't be treated cruelly or unfairly. Even then you had rights under the law.

Of course you take all this for granted now. But except in England and the countries settled by England, like America and Canada and Australia, it is all quite new. Even today there is no such thing as fair play, or fair trial, in many of the countries of the world. Even today in Russia and Hungary and Spain and China, men and women go around in fear of their lives. They never know when there may be a knock on the door and the secret police will march in and take one of them off to jail. And nothing to do about it! And as for fair trial—why, that is nonsense. Dictators have no time for fair trial. Besides, if they were willing to allow fair trials, they wouldn't be dictators. No, no . . . bring the prisoner in, charge him with some crime, it makes no difference what, beat him if he makes trouble, torture him to get a confession, then sentence him to prison for twenty or thirty years, and that is the end of him. That will teach people to be independent; that will teach them to make trouble!

The English won fair trial early, but for most other people it was a long time coming, and it took much bloodshed and tragedy and misery before it came.

Take France, for instance.

Remember the Huguenots—how they were forced to escape from France and find asylum in other countries if they wanted to keep their religion?

Of course many of them stayed on in France. They went "underground," as we would say today—that is, they kept up their religion in secret. A dangerous thing, that, for the government, and the Church got more and more determined to wipe out the Huguenots, and more and more merciless about the methods they used.

Here is one Huguenot minister caught with his prayer books and his Bible; he was hanged. And three brothers who tried to defend him when he was captured; all of them had their heads chopped off. Here is another poor devil: he gave lodging to a Huguenot minister for one night; for that he was sent to the galleys for twenty years—chained to a seat in the great ships, bending his back to the oars day after day, until he dropped dead of weariness and pain.

No mercy for the Huguenots. They were a bad lot, and no need to give them "justice." The only justice was to get rid of them! Just what Cortez had said when he killed off all the Aztec Indians of Mexico. . . . Just what Pizarro had said when he wiped out the Inca Indians of Peru. They were all heathens; they didn't deserve justice. . . . Just what the Turks said when they murdered half a million Armenians. . . . Just the way Hitler argued, a few years ago, when he killed off all the Jews he could lay his hands on: they were Jews and didn't deserve justice.

That's the way the King and the judges reasoned in France in the years after the flight of the Huguenots—that is, in the reigns of Louis XIV and Louis XV.

Look at what happened to a Huguenot named Jean Calas, down in Toulouse in the south of France.

Everybody respected Jean Calas and his family: a proper, law-abiding man, an honest shopkeeper, a good husband and father, a good master, a good citizen. Of course they knew that he was a Huguenot, but as long as he didn't bother anybody, they overlooked that.

But, alas, Calas had a son who was always in trouble, who always managed to fail at all the things he wanted most to do. And one dreadful day the son went off and hanged himself.

What a shocking thing to happen. A suicide couldn't get a proper burial. His body would be dragged through the streets and then hung on the gallows. A suicide disgraced his name and his family. . . . So the father said that it was all an accident—his poor son had fallen and killed himself.

Here at last was a chance to punish old man Calas for being a Protestant.

No such thing, said the Court. The death of young Marc Calas wasn't an accident at all. He wasn't a suicide either. It was murder!

Jean Calas had killed his son, said the Court. He had killed the boy to prevent him from turning Catholic. That was the real story!

It was a religious murder, said the Court. And old Jean Calas must suffer for it.

Now the whole of Toulouse was in an uproar. In the past they had liked old Calas and his family well enough, but now they were swept by terror and hatred. Public opinion can change like that; it can swing around, just like the wind, and for no reason.

So Jean Calas was arrested and dragged off to jail and charged with the murder of his son. Then he was tried for that terrible crime.

*Fair trial!* Why, nobody thought of that for a moment. Fair trial for a Huguenot? Fair trial for a murderer? Nonsense.

What followed was a mockery of a trial.

First the old man was tortured to make him confess. That proved useless, for he didn't confess. Then the judges advertised for people to come and bear witness against Calas. Come one, come all, tell anything you want, make any accusations you can think of—the worse they are the more the judges will thank you. And as for those who tried to speak up and say a good word for Calas—why, they were seized and thrown into prison just as if they had been criminals themselves.

Really the whole trial was just a pretense, for the judges had made up their minds in advance, and even written their decision in advance. They knew that Calas was guilty, and that was the end of the matter. Why bother with evidence? Why bother with a hearing? Why bother with a fair trial?

So the Court sat in judgment on Calas and said he was guilty.

Poor old Calas, was there ever so pitiful an old man? First to lose his son. Then to see his family scattered to the winds, his wife and children in hiding, his house and all his belongings taken from him. Then to be put to torture—the worst kind of torture that the judges could think of. They tied him to a great wheel and broke all his bones, one by one. They poured gallons and gallons of water down his throat. They left him out in the sun to die in agony.

All that was to make him confess to his crime. But he never confessed. After all, he was innocent.

Now Jean Calas was dead, and his wife and his daughters were in hiding, and his other son had somehow escaped across the mountains to Geneva in Switzerland. It was all over—the trial and punishment of Calas.

No, it wasn't all over. History is never really all over, and nothing is settled until it is settled right.

Look! Over in Geneva the young Donat Calas has thrown himself on the mercy of the great Voltaire.

Now we come to Voltaire. He is worth staying with for a time; indeed he is worth staying with for a whole lifetime.

He had a resounding name: François Marie Arouet de Voltaire. He had been a dashing young man, but now he was a little old man with a face like a fox and a skin as wrinkled as a prune, and eyes that mocked at you, and a mind that worked twice as fast as any other mind in Europe, and a heart that was at least twice as big. . . . He lived in a splendid house at Ferney, just outside the city of Geneva—a house with a dozen splendid rooms and a private theater, and a great library, and lovely gardens running down to the blue Lake of Geneva, and when he looked out of his windows he could see the sun dancing on the waters of the lake and the snow-capped mountains pointing up into the sky. The rooms were for the many guests who crowded in on him from all over Europe. The theater was to put on the plays that he wrote. The library was for his own books. He hadn't written *all* of them, to be sure, but sometimes it seemed as if he had. One day you will read some of his books, but don't plan to read them all unless you have lots of time on your hands, for there are almost a hundred volumes.

Voltaire—the name that was feared and loved more than any name of his time. The sharpest tongue and the sharpest wit in all Europe—a tongue that could lash out like the tongue of a scorpion and sting as badly; a pen that flashed like a sword, and cut too. There was really nothing that

Voltaire couldn't do, and nothing that he wouldn't do, either, for that matter, if he thought he ought. Nothing frightened him—not kings nor bishops nor judges. They had put him in jail, they had beaten him, they had banished him, they had burned his books—all to no avail. Voltaire spoke his mind no matter where he was and no matter what the issue was. And what a mind! He wrote all the best histories, and the King, who detested him, nevertheless had to make him the royal historian because to make anybody else that would have been ridiculous. He wrote philosophy, he wrote politics, he wrote fables and tales, he wrote poetry, he wrote plays. And, like Thomas Jefferson, whom he resembled in so many ways, he wrote thousands of letters, and almost every one of them planted a new idea in the mind of the reader. Voltaire's France was teeming with writers and historians and philosophers, and every one of them looked to Voltaire and called him master.

For Voltaire was the brightest star in the firmament of France. He was the sun around which all the other stars circled. Talk about Louis XIV being the Sun King—why, Voltaire outshone even kings. Certainly he outshone poor simple-minded Louis XV, who did his best to get rid of the troublesome Voltaire. But you could no more get rid of Voltaire than you could get rid of the weather. Frederick the Great of Prussia, who was twice as important as Louis XV, admired Voltaire so much he even managed to look like him. He had Voltaire come and live with him for three years, and he would have kept him forever, if he could. And in St. Petersburg, in Russia, the Empress Catherine—who was also called the Great—sent letter after letter asking Voltaire to come and stay with her and be honored, and spoiled, by her court.

But Voltaire would have none of that. What he wanted was independence. He didn't need to live at a court; wherever he lived was a court. He had money enough for all his needs—after all, everybody in Europe bought his books and watched his plays. He built himself two houses outside Geneva, and another in Lausanne, so no matter which king tried to arrest him or make trouble for him—which king or which city or state—he could always slip off to one of his houses in another state and be safe.

What side was he on, this Voltaire, with all his genius and his brilliance and his spirit? He was on the side of liberty. He was on the side of justice. He was on the side of humanity. That's why Louis XV was so afraid of him. That's why the Church in France was so afraid of him. He could always be counted on to speak out against wrong and expose injustice, and to arouse the conscience of Europe on behalf of the right.

No wonder young Donat Calas turned to Voltaire for help. The old man—he was deep into his sixties then—listened to the boy's story with wonder and with horror. Could such things really be, in France, in the 1760s? "I shall drop this matter only with my death," he said. "Since the massacre of St. Bartholomew nothing has so disgraced the human spirit as the murder of Calas. . . . Cry out! Cry out! for Calas."

Cry out he did, and his voice was heard all over Europe. The judges down in Toulouse who thought they had buried Calas forever had reckoned without Voltaire. Now everybody was talking about the Calas case—in Switzerland, in England, in France. . . . Now all Voltaire's friends up in Paris were clamoring for the Court to reopen the case.

"No!" said the judges. "Never!" said the judges. "Impossible!" said the judges. "The case is over. Calas is dead, and we are content."

Then Voltaire put everything aside and bent all his genius to the task of getting justice for Calas. How the letters went streaming out, to the great and the powerful up in Paris, to lawyers and judges, to writers and editors. "The honor of France is at stake," wrote Voltaire, "the honor of mankind is at stake. The case must be reopened." The clamor rose higher and higher; all France joined in and then all Europe, and at last even the King could no longer resist it. He ordered the case of Calas to be reopened.

Of course, once that was done, the whole case fell apart. Once impartial judges got a look at the facts and the papers, it was clear that there was no case against old Jean Calas at all. It was like the Emperor's new clothes in Hans Christian Andersen's story: there weren't any clothes. There was no reason to suppose that the Calas boy had ever been murdered at all. There was no reason in the world to put any blame on his father. The whole case was a tissue of lies, from beginning to end.

So Calas was cleared . . . poor Calas, tortured to death there in Toulouse. His family could come home again and have their house and their belongings back. The judges were all very sorry. Everybody was very sorry. . . . But there was nothing to do about it now.

That's what happens when you don't have fair trial.

Now cross the Atlantic Ocean to America. From the beginning the Americans had been part of England, and they had been brought up on the Great Charter and on fair trial. When they came to write their own constitutions, some of them in 1776 and some in 1787, they wrote fair trial into them. No man to be imprisoned except by the law of the land; everyone to have his day in court; trial by jury; everyone innocent until proved guilty; no cruel punishments . . . all the familiar guarantees. They were all in the Bills of Rights, and everybody was safe.

How proud Americans were of their Bill of Rights. In America *everybody* was sure of a fair trial.

Everybody? Certainly all the great and the powerful; certainly all ordinary men and women too. But how about the poor and the friendless? How about Negroes?

One summer day in 1837 a Portuguese pirate ship named the *Tecora* sailed into the harbor of Havana, in the island of Cuba. A *real* pirate ship, like Captain Kidd's? Well, not quite. But a pirate ship all the same. For the *Tecora* carried a cargo of Negroes stolen from their homes in Africa, and the captain of the *Tecora* was going to sell the Africans as slaves.

In the eyes of the law the slave trade was piracy, and the *Tecora* was a pirate ship.

But that didn't bother the Portuguese captain, who made a tidy profit selling the Africans as slaves. Nor did it bother the two Cubans, Señor Ruiz and Señor Montez, who bought the Africans and sailed off with them on another ship named the *Amistad* to sell them to Cuban sugar planters.

They had done this so many times now, Señor Ruiz and Señor Montez, and it never occurred to them that there was anything unusual about it this time. But there was. The Africans were unusual. They were of the Mendi tribe, from Sierra Leone, a tribe not used to slavery. And their leader was unusual too. He was a young chieftain named Cinque, handsome, intelligent, and fearless.

After the long terrible trip across the ocean the Mendi were in a dangerous mood. And their mood became more dangerous every day. Just for taking a drink of water the captain of the *Amistad* flogged one of the Africans until the poor fellow ran with blood, and then he rubbed salt into the wounds. . . . Four days out on the *Amistad*, and Cinque and his fellow Africans broke the great iron chain that bound them, and cut the ropes around their feet. Then they found some of the great knives used to cut sugar cane, attacked the Cuban captain and crew, killed two of them, and overpowered the others. . . . Now they were free! But what good did that do them? They couldn't sail the ship, after all; they didn't know one rope from another. "We will spare your lives if you steer our ship back to Africa," they told Señores Ruiz and Montez.

Of course the two Cubans agreed. And of course they did no such thing. By day they sailed east, toward Africa; by night they sailed west, back to America. Then, at last, they headed for the United States. Late in August they reached Long Island, off New York. There Cinque put ashore for water, and quickly the word went around that there was a strange ship, with a strange crew—a kind of ghost ship—in the waters off New York. Within a few days an American naval ship took the *Amistad* in tow and escorted it into harbor and lodged all the Africans in jail in the city of New Haven.

Now everything seemed to happen at once. Ruiz and Montez told how they had been attacked and how their companions had been murdered by the Negroes. What a frightful story! To jail, then, with the terrible Cinque and his little army of followers, until they could be properly punished. But Ruiz and Montez didn't want them in jail. They wanted their slaves back again so they could sell them and pocket the profits. . . . And now the Spanish minister comes into the picture—remember that Cuba belonged to Spain in those days. The minister wanted all the Africans sent back to Havana so that he could make an example of them. "Just wait till we get our hands on them," he said; "hanging is too good for them!"

Things certainly looked black for Cinque and his fellow Africans.

But not so fast.

Here and there men were looking up and taking an interest in the poor Mendi Negroes. They couldn't speak a word of English and nobody could understand their language, so it was hard to get their story. But wasn't there something fishy about the whole thing?

That's what Lewis Tappan thought, down in New York City; he was a rich merchant, and an abolitionist, and he had the same nose for injustice that a hunting dog has for a 'possum. That's what Ellis Gray Loring thought up in

Boston; he was a lawyer who spent all his spare time and money taking care of those nobody else would take care of. And that's what some of the professors at Yale College thought too, especially the famous Josiah Gibbs. He was so clever he could figure out almost any language, and in no time at all he had learned enough Mendi to talk with Cinque and his companions and to get their story.

So, what with everybody helping, the real story came out.

The *Amistad* Africans weren't slaves at all. They were free men who had been kidnaped out of Africa and shipped into slavery. That was against the law, and the law said that anyone who stole Negroes for slaves should suffer death.

All right, then; the Africans weren't slaves. Still, that wasn't the end of the story. After all, they had killed the captain and sailed off with the ship. Didn't that make them thieves and murderers?

Not at all, said their friends. After all, if they weren't slaves but free men, they had a right to rise up against their kidnapers and to win their freedom.

The main thing was to see to it that they weren't bundled off to Cuba, or to Spain, where they would certainly be punished and—those who were left, anyway—sold into slavery. The main thing was to be sure that they had a fair trial.

Fair trial. Fair trial for the Mendi Africans. Fair trial for slaves. After all, that was the only way to find out if they really were slaves.

So there was to be a trial, and in the Supreme Court of the United States, too, with the whole country looking on.

Who would speak for the Africans?

John Quincy Adams. Son of President John Adams. Senator from the state of Massachusetts. Secretary of State of the United States. President of the United States. The greatest man in the country, the man who had done more for his country than any man alive in 1840.

Now he was seventy-three years old. His hand trembled when he wrote; his eyes filled with tears; his voice quavered; he couldn't trust his memory or even his mind. Anyway that's what *he* said. Nobody else said that. Even those who hated him most—and down South they sat up nights just to hate John Quincy Adams—admitted that at seventy-three Old Man Eloquent was worth two of anybody else.

When Adams was a young man—really just a boy—over in England with his father, he went to see the Great Charter of 1215. How his heart beat when he looked down at the signatures at the end of it and saw the name Saer de Quency.

His ancestor. He was sure of it!

The Quincys had been on the side of liberty for six hundred years. That was a great heritage. He could not fail it now.

So old John Quincy Adams took on the defense of the *Amistad* Negroes. First, then, down to New Haven, where they had already languished in jail for almost two years, to talk with them. . . . They got along famously, the old man and the young Africans; and when Adams reached Washington a few days later there was a letter for him from one of the Mendi. "Dear friend Mr. Adams," it said. "You have children and friends, you love them, you feel very sorry if Mendi people come and take them to Africa. . . . We never kill captain if he no kill us. If Court ask who bring Mendi people, we bring ourselves. All we want is make us free."

"All we want is make us free"—there's the cry of all people, in all ages of history.

Well, Adams would do his best.

Then came the trial. Picture the scene—the old courtroom with its marble pillars, in the basement of the Senate. Eight black-robed judges sitting up there on the bench—

there should have been nine, but one of them had just died —and in the middle of them the Chief Justice, Mr. Taney, with his long thin face and his noble forehead and his eyes as sharp as diamonds. Next to him Judge Joseph Story—the man who had been appointed to the Supreme Court when Adams himself refused the appointment, so in a sense he was sitting in Adams' place. . . . Story knew everything there was to know; he had read all the books of law ever written—and he had written a good many of them himself. He was not only a judge but a professor at the Harvard Law School, and half a dozen other things as well. Anyway he was the greatest judge in America, and some people thought he was the greatest judge in the world.

And there, pleading for the Africans, was Old Man Eloquent.

The Supreme Court of the United States and the man who had been President of the United States, all to see that the Africans had a fair trial.

"I had been deeply distressed till the moment when I arose," wrote Adams in his diary, "and then my spirit did not sink within me. . . . I did not answer to public expectations, but I have not utterly failed."

As he spoke the years fell away from the old man, all the fire and passion of his youth came back to him. Hour after hour he went on, it took two days for him to complete his argument. And when he was through? Well . . . "I have not utterly failed," he wrote, and indeed he had not. Judge Story read the opinion of the Court. The Africans had never been slaves. The Africans had a right to fight for their freedom. The Africans were free.

Fair trial.

Now back to France. Not the same France. There had been a Revolution; there had been a Napoleon Bonaparte. There had been an Empire. Now there was a Republic and a Constitution, and even a Bill of Rights. Had France learned about fair trial since Voltaire cried out for Calas?

The year was 1894 and once again there was a trial. Captain Alfred Dreyfus was on trial for treason.

The army said that Captain Dreyfus sold secrets to the Germans. They were ready to prove that Captain Dreyfus was a traitor, and to put the blame for everything that had gone wrong in the army for years squarely on the shoulders of Dreyfus. Why? Because he was a Jew, and the men who ran the army still hadn't learned that Jews are people, too, and that Jews have the same rights as everyone else.

Was it a fair trial? Not at all. It was almost as unfair as the trial of Jean Calas more than a hundred years earlier. No torture this time, to be sure, no breaking on the wheel, no persecution of the family. But what happened was almost as bad.

It was a secret trial. Nobody on the outside was allowed to know what went on. Why? "Reasons of state" . . . "reasons of security" . . . a good excuse, that, for secrecy. Captain Dreyfus was not allowed to see the evidence against him or to ask questions of those who bore witness against him. He was not even allowed to defend himself properly. Who could doubt the outcome of such a trial? Of course the Court found Captain Dreyfus guilty of treason. They stripped him of his army rank, his uniform, and his decorations, and sent him off to Devil's Island, for the rest of his life.

Devil's Island—just a barren rock off the coast of South America. It deserved its name, too. You were better off dead, than alive on Devil's Island. They put Dreyfus—he was no longer Captain Dreyfus—in a little hut all by himself, and fastened a chain to one of his ankles, and then put a guard outside his hut just as if he were really dangerous or might escape. For a long time they didn't let him have any letters or see any friends, or talk with anyone. During the day he could walk for a few hundred feet back and forth on his rocky island, and at night he tried to sleep in his hut, with a lamp burning all night long and the insects buzzing around the lamp. . . .

Meanwhile back in Paris the generals all sighed with relief. They had put the blame for everything on that troublesome Jew. And with the newspapers to help them, they had whipped up anger against the Jews, and had the people on their side. Now they were stronger than ever, these generals—stronger even than the government.

But wait.

There was a Voltaire for Dreyfus, too.

His name was Emile Zola. Like Voltaire, he was a man of letters—a journalist, a novelist. He was one of the great novelists of his time.

When Zola heard how Captain Dreyfus had been tried and sentenced and shipped off to Devil's Island, his soul was stirred. He didn't know whether Dreyfus was guilty or innocent. But he did know that Dreyfus had not had a fair trial. That was enough.

"I accuse!" he wrote.

"I accuse the army of injustice . . . of the persecution of Dreyfus because he is a Jew. I accuse the courts of injustice. I accuse the newspapers of injustice. I accuse the French people of injustice . . . of denying Dreyfus a fair trial because he is a Jew."

And now another voice took up the charge. It was the voice of a man named Georges Clemenceau.

He, too, was stirred by this example of injustice.

Here he stood, at the threshold of a great career. Before he was through he would be Prime Minister of France. He would lead France through the First World War to victory. He would go down in history as "The Tiger" because of his ferocious courage.

Now he was already showing that courage. He stood up against the army and the Court and the government, and he, too, said, "I accuse you of denying Dreyfus a fair trial because he is a Jew."

All of France was rocked by the Dreyfus case. And not France alone: the whole of Europe was stirred. Never had there been such a case. Was Dreyfus a traitor . . . or was he an innocent victim of a gigantic plot against him? France had to know. The world had to know.

So in 1899 they brought Dreyfus back from Devil's Island for another trial . . . Dreyfus who had no idea what a stir he was making in the world. This second trial was a bit better than the first, but it still wasn't a fair trial. The government still hadn't learned its lesson. Once again the Court said that Dreyfus was guilty, but it was clear to everybody that this time they weren't at all sure of it. And this time, too, everybody could see that there had not been a fair trial.

The clamor rose louder and louder, and beat against the government like giant ocean waves dashing themselves on the shore.

Now the government was in a panic.

The officers who had charged Dreyfus with treason were in a panic. One of them killed himself. Another ran away to England and went into hiding.

So now there had to be a third trial.

This time it was a fair trial. This time nothing was secret and nothing was covered up for reasons of "national security." This time Dreyfus knew what all the charges were, and had a chance to look at all the evidence and to defend himself.

And of course the whole case against him crumbled into dust, just as the case against Calas had crumbled into dust. It all turned out to be nothing. Someone had sold secrets to the Germans, but it was not Dreyfus; in fact it was the man who had first accused him. All the evidence against Dreyfus had been forged. The "reasons of security" weren't reasons at all—they were just ways for the army to cover up the fact that it didn't really have a case.

Now no one in his senses doubted that Dreyfus was innocent.

And now everybody was sorry. Now, more than ten years later, Captain Dreyfus was given back his uniform and his rank and his decorations, and given some more decorations to make up for all that he had suffered. And now everybody shouted "*Vive Dreyfus! Vive la justice!*"

Long live Dreyfus: yes, of course. But he couldn't live forever.

Long live justice: yes. Justice can live forever.

# THE DECLARATION OF HUMAN RIGHTS

What a spectacle it is, when we look back upon it, this long, desperate, heartbreaking struggle to be free. The struggle of men and women to throw off the bonds of slavery. The never ending struggle for the right to speak. The magnificent struggle for the right to worship God. The struggle to work out of the blackness of ignorance. The struggle for the rights of life and happiness, for the rights of women and of children. . . . This it is that makes the whole world one. This it is that ties together centuries of history into a kind of unity—this struggle to be free, this struggle toward the light. This it is that brings together mothers in Norway and India—the fact that they want their children to go to school. This it is that brings together the men and women of Japan and of Israel: that they want to worship God in their own way. This it is that brings together Negroes of South Africa and of the Congo and the Arab peoples of Egypt and the Hindus of India: that they want the same chance at freedom and happiness that the white peoples of Europe and America have so long enjoyed. And this it is that unites the heroes of all nations—heroes of freedom of religion like Roger Williams, of freedom from slavery like the American Frederick Douglass and the Haitian Toussaint L'Ouverture, and of freedom of asylum like Fridtjof Nansen, and of freedom for women and children like Jane Addams.

When you look back on that long story of struggle you cannot but believe there is something very deep in the heart of man which demands freedom.

That is the first lesson, then, that all men are bound together by the strongest of ties—the love of freedom. But there is another side to this. Those who do not have freedom are bound together too.

Every one of you who reads this book already enjoys freedom—otherwise you wouldn't be reading it. You have freedom to read, freedom to learn, freedom to think. . . . You are all bound together by good fortune. But there are millions and millions of people all over the world who do not have freedom. They do not have the right to read or to speak their minds; they do not have the right to work at the things that interest them. . . . They do not even have freedom from injustice or freedom from fear.

Are they your business?

Remember the story of Abel and Cain in the Old Testament, in which Cain asked, "Am I my brother's keeper?"

The answer is easy. Of course—we are all our brothers' keepers.

You wouldn't stand by stuffing yourself with food while children who were starving stretched out their hands to you in pitiful appeal. You wouldn't say, "It's none of my business," and go on eating.

You wouldn't stand by and see some little boy beaten by a big bully—and say, "It's none of my business."

You wouldn't enjoy being waited on by other children—who were slaves.

You wouldn't even enjoy your own schools—the shining new cafeterias, the well-stocked libraries, the gymnasium, and the swimming pool—if you could look out of the windows and see ragged children working in factories across the street.

Of course not. None of us would. We would all share what we had to eat; we would step in and fight the bully; we would wait on ourselves; we would try to bring the working children into our schools and playgrounds.

That's easy enough—when they are right there before our eyes. It's a bit harder when all these things are a thousand miles away. . . . It's harder to take in, then, that there *are* millions of children who are starving; that there *are* millions of men and women who are being bullied by soldiers or by the police; that there *are* millions of people who are still slaves; that there *are* millions of children working in the fields and the factories instead of going to school.

It takes some imagination to think of all these as if they were right there in front of us. But then it takes imagination for almost anything that is important.

There is another thing to remember, too, when we contrast our own good fortune with the hard times that so many other people suffer—the misery and poverty, the ignorance, the tyranny, the slavery that still go on in so many parts of the globe.

It is this:

Poverty, ignorance, tyranny, slavery—these things are all like contagious diseases. It's no good saying that it's all right as long as *we* can read, or as long as *we* are free to worship as we please, or as long as *we* can speak our minds, or join labor unions, or be sure of a fair trial, or as long as *we* have enough to eat. Slavery and tyranny, like measles and smallpox, are catching. The people who are not allowed to read newspapers or hear the radio, who are not allowed to go to school, who are not allowed to have a fair trial—these carry their ignorance and their fears and anger around with them, and spread them. The people who are poor and hungry and miserable spread their envies and their hatreds and their greeds. . . .

Just as a disease will spread from house to house and town to town, so poverty and injustice spread from people to people and from country to country. Trouble in Cuba means trouble all over South America—and in the United States too. Warfare and terror in the Congo mean trouble all over Africa—and in Europe and America too. If the white people of South Africa or of Alabama are unjust to the colored people, that injustice is felt by colored people everywhere in the world. If the little children of India haven't enough to eat, if the children of Bolivia don't go to school, if the children of the Arab countries are sickly and crippled, sooner or later the children of Denmark and Canada and Australia will feel the bad effects.

Three hundred years ago a great poet put this as well as it has ever been put. "No man," he said, "is an island entire of itself; every man is a piece of the Continent. . . . Any man's death diminishes me, because I am involved in Mankind."

All of us are involved in mankind. Whatever hurts other people hurts us, too, and in very real and practical ways, like the spread of slums in the big cities. It hurts us, too, in moral ways. For if it is bad not to share your food with a starving child who stands in front of you, it is just as bad not to help starving children in distant India. If it is cowardly not to try to help one boy when he is attacked by a gang of bullies, it is just as cowardly not to help men who are attacked by bullies or soldiers in South Africa. We have to help people everywhere, for their sakes, and for our own sakes as well, because we are all "involved in Mankind."

There's another thing about all these rights we have been discussing. They are all tied together. Each one of them is part of a network of rights. When you stop to think of it, that is not at all surprising; it is the common sense of the matter. Think how all your own rights (you don't call them that, of course, because you take them for granted) are all tied together: the right to go to school, the right to read, to talk, to play, to have enough to eat—all of these are part of your way of living.

All our rights are not only tied together; they are dependent on each other.

It's no use being free to say whatever you want, if you haven't anything to say.

It's no use being free to read, if you can't read.

It's no use being free to work at whatever job you like best, if there aren't any jobs at all.

And all the freedom in the world won't help you if you are driven out of your country and can't find asylum anywhere.

You must have noticed, as you read these stories of human rights, that many of the leading characters could have shifted their roles about from one story to another with the greatest of ease. After all, Tom Paine belongs in the story of freedom of religion, or of fair trial, or of asylum, as well as in the story of free speech. Theodore Parker, too, belongs in the story of free speech or freedom of religion just as much as in the story of the struggle against slavery. Jane Addams plays a leading role in the struggle for the rights of children, the rights of women, fair trial, the struggle for peace, the right of asylum—almost everything. Or look at the story of the Huguenots. We told that story as part of the right of asylum. But it is a chapter in the history of religious freedom because the Huguenots were not allowed to worship as they wished. It is a chapter in the story of free speech, because the Huguenots were silenced. It is a chapter in the story of fair trial, as we know from the history of the pitiful Jean Calas. . . . And so it goes with every one of these.

The destinies of all people are connected. All human rights are connected.

These are like some giant net. The strands that go one way are made up of people; the strands that go the other way are made up of their rights. And each one is tied together with all the others by a hundred knots. Cut the net in any one place, cut the knots that tie up people to their rights, and the whole net will unravel.

The only way to make sure that people are safe and that rights are safe is to tie all the knots firmly. The only way to make sure that everybody has fair play is to make all the rights universal.

That is what the United Nations is trying to do.

Even while the great war against Hitler was still raging, President Franklin D. Roosevelt was thinking and planning for the world that was ahead.

How were the people of the world to avoid another war —a war which might wipe them all out of existence? How were they to avoid those injustices and fears and hatreds that make wars?

Out of President Roosevelt's thinking and planning, and the thinking and planning of hundreds of other men and women in many countries, came the United Nations.

The United Nations has two grand purposes—just as all governments have two grand purposes.

The first purpose is to keep order and keep the peace.

The second purpose is to take care of the welfare of ordinary men and women.

In 1945, out in San Francisco, spokesmen for fifty countries came together and created the United Nations. Soon it moved to New York, and it grew and grew, until today it has one hundred members. . . . If you go to New York you will visit it: the tall gleaming building, on the shore of the East River, the great library and the conference buildings; the splendid meeting halls with their handsome wall paintings; the hundreds of delegates from all countries, many of them dressed in their native costumes, thronging the corridors and sitting rooms. . . . There it is, the great monument to peace.

But the United Nations does more than try to keep the peace. It does a hundred other things as well. It feeds hungry children and teaches farmers how to grow more grain; it stamps out dangerous diseases; acts as a court of law when nations quarrel with each other; sets standards of work—hours and conditions of work—all around the globe; wipes out illiteracy. . . . What does the United Nations not do?

But what of rights? What of the rights of man?

How was the United Nations to see to it that men and women everywhere were secure in their freedoms? What could it do to protect them in the exercise of their rights?

That's what people were asking all over the world—the men and women who had been fighting for long years for their rights and for the rights of their fellow men.

What of the rights of man?

That is what Eleanor Roosevelt was asking.

Nobody in our time has done more for the rights of men and women and children than Mrs. Roosevelt. No one has had the freedom of the peoples of the earth more closely at heart.

Eleanor Roosevelt is one of those wonderful people who could fit into any one of the chapters in the story of human rights. Free speech? She has always championed the right of the poor and neglected to speak their minds. Once she tried to speak in a town owned by a coal-mining company. They had forbidden her to speak on their land, so she went to the United States Post Office and stood on the steps there and gave her speech. That was United States property and nobody could stop free speech there. Mrs. Roosevelt thought that every spot on earth ought to be just that free.

Was it the rights of women and children? All her life, from the time she was a young social worker in the slums of

New York City, Eleanor Roosevelt has taken special care of women and children. She is like Jane Addams; she thinks that women should have all the rights of men and that children should have all the rights and all the love that there is to have.

Was it freedom from slavery? She has gone all over the world—to every continent and almost every country—seeking out those who were oppressed and abused, and speaking up for them, pleading their cause, helping them out into the bright light of freedom. And everywhere in the world she is known and loved because she thinks that all men and women, of all colors and races, are equal in the sight of God and should have equal rights.

When she was a little girl her grandmother used to say to her: "Eleanor, you are a girl, and I expect you to be more sensible and more thoughtful than your brothers." More was expected of girls than of boys; more was expected of women than of men: she learned that from the beginning and she has acted on that belief all her life.

She learned something else, too. Remember how people like Fridtjof Nansen and Jane Addams and Charles Brace felt that they had a special obligation to the poor and the unfortunate just because they were so well off and so fortunate? Mrs. Roosevelt felt that too.

For Eleanor Roosevelt, like so many of the champions of the poor and the oppressed—like Wendell Phillips and Jane Addams—was born lucky. She belonged to one of New York's great families; when she was still a little girl her uncle Theodore was President of the United States. She was educated by governesses and in English schools; she traveled in England and all over Europe. When she came home it was to marry her handsome cousin Franklin—everybody knew that he was a young man with a great future. That meant that in time she was the wife of the governor of New York; then the wife of the President of the United States—the only President to be elected more than twice. . . . Between the two of them, her uncle and her husband, the Roosevelts were in the White House for twenty years!

Eleanor Roosevelt—now we should call her Mrs. Roosevelt—was born to be First Lady—the First Lady of the United States and, in time, the First Lady of the world.

What was it that made her the protector of the poor and the oppressed in every land? What was it that made her the spokesman for all those who had no other spokesmen? What was it that made her the champion of peace and of justice everywhere?

More than anything else, it was the fact that she never thought of herself. She never thought that she was important. She never thought what kind of a figure she would cut. There was no work that was too ordinary for her—she was like Jane Addams in that: she would dandle babies on her knee, or make lemonade at a children's party, or drive long hours to little towns where she addressed some youth encampment. Never was there a more unselfish crusader. She treated everybody alike; if she made tea for the Queen of England she could make it for a group of Girl Scouts who came to call on her; if she could speak to the great of the world in the United Nations, she could speak at some high school in Oklahoma. Her whole life reminds us of that wonderful line from the English poet George Herbert:

*Who sweeps a room, as for Thy laws,*
*Makes that and th' action fine.*

The United Nations would not be complete until it had done something to protect the rights of men and women in all lands: that much was clear.

What to do?

President Truman asked Mrs. Roosevelt to represent the United States in the new United Nations, and of course she agreed—she always agreed to do whatever looked like her duty. And besides, she thought, what a chance to strike a blow for the rights of man!

That's just what the other delegates to the United Nations thought too: what a chance for the rights of man. Put Mrs. Roosevelt on the job. . . . And they did. In no time at all she was giving most of her time to human rights. The United Nations decided to draw up a Declaration of Human Rights, and they made Mrs. Roosevelt chairman of the committee to draw up the Declaration.

What *were* the rights of man?

Not as easy as you might think, that question. Just think how hard it is to get white people and Negroes in Mississippi to agree on basic rights. Think how hard it is to get members of a labor union and their employers to agree on basic rights. Yet they all live in the same country, they have all gone to the same schools, they have all studied the same Bill of Rights. Then think how hard it is to get Americans and Russians, Frenchmen and Algerians, Israelis and Egyptians, to agree on basic rights!

But Mrs. Roosevelt was firm and patient, and kept everlastingly at it. No matter how much the members of her committee wrangled, she never seemed to get tired or angry. Sometimes she kept the delegates there for hours on end, until they finally hammered out some kind of agreements. The Russians wanted one thing, the Indians another, the Africans still another. . . . And everything had to be translated into English and French—Mrs. Roosevelt found herself even doing that—and then it had to be explained and discussed and discussed and explained.

But gradually it all took shape. As Mrs. Roosevelt and her committee moved back and forth from New York to Geneva, from Geneva to Paris, from Paris back to New York, the members learned to understand one another and to realize that they had common purposes. After all, the sentiment for fair play is pretty much the same everywhere in the world, and much of human rights comes down to that: fair play.

In the end the committee came up with:

## A UNIVERSAL DECLARATION OF HUMAN RIGHTS

What did it say?

All human beings are born free and equal
All have the rights of life and liberty and security
All are free; none are slaves
All are equal in the eyes of the law
All must have a fair trial
All have the right to privacy
All are free to travel
All have a right of asylum
All have a right to marry and raise a family
All have a right to own property
All have a right to free thought and to free speech
All have a right to worship freely
All have a right to join—or not to join—clubs and parties
All have the right to take part in the politics and government of their country
All have a right to work at fair wages
All have a right to join trade unions
All have a right to rest and to play
All have a right to food and drink, clothes and shelter
All have a right to security in sickness or in old age
All have a right to an education in school and out of school

What a long list.

It adds up to something pretty familiar—to the rights that Thomas Jefferson wrote into the Declaration of Independence: Life, Liberty and the Pursuit of Happiness.

So now there was a universal Bill of Rights.

First—remember?—there had been the Great Charter of 1215.

Then came the charters of freedom in America and in England—the Massachusetts Body of Liberties in 1641, and the English Bill of Rights in 1689, and then the famous Bills of Rights of Virginia and Massachusetts and all the other states, and then the Bill of Rights in the United States

Constitution. Then the French caught the idea and had their own Declaration of the Rights of Man—Jefferson helped write it—and after that almost all of the new states that came swimming into history, in Europe and South America, added their Bills of Rights.

Now at last, in the year 1948, a Bill of Rights for all people everywhere in the world.

Now we are through.

With this book. Yes. Books must come to an end.

With this story. No. A story like this never comes to an end. You can't win human rights once and for all—as you win a baseball game, for instance. They have to be won over and over again. "*Eternal* vigilance is the price of liberty"—yes, eternal vigilance. Even in free countries like the United States or France or India the rights of man are always in danger. Even in these countries there are always some who do not really believe in human rights—anyway, not for other people. Even here there are some who want to silence free speech, or deny the vote to Negroes, or refuse freedom of worship to those they dislike.

And, besides, there are always new rights to be won. There is a great universe of human rights to be explored—it is like the universe of space, it is like the universe of science. We can never hope to know everything about space or to conquer the whole of it. We can never hope to learn all the secrets of science. We can never hope to exhaust all the beauty of the world, or all the philosophy. And we can never hope to master all rights, all freedoms.

There are always new worlds to conquer.

VIENNA, AUSTRIA
MARCH 15

AMHERST, MASS.
MAY 15

# INDEX

ASHAWAY FREE LIBRARY
3 5988 00013 7856

WITHDRAWN